THE WAY PEOPLE LIVE

Life in the Australian Outback

Titles in The Way People Live series include:

Cowboys in the Old West
Games of Ancient Rome
Life Among the Great Plains Indians
Life Among the Ibo Women of Nigeria
Life Among the Indian Fighters
Life Among the Pirates
Life Among the Puritans
Life Among the Samurai
Life Among the Vikings
Life During the Black Death
Life During the Crusades
Life During the French Revolution
Life During the Gold Rush
Life During the Great Depression
Life During the Middle Ages
Life During the Renaissance
Life During the Russian Revolution
Life During the Spanish Inquisition
Life in a California Mission
Life in a Japanese American
   Internment Camp
Life in a Medieval Castle
Life in a Medieval Monastery
Life in America During the 1960s
Life in an Amish Community
Life in a Nazi Concentration Camp
Life in Ancient Athens
Life in Ancient China
Life in Ancient Egypt
Life in Ancient Greece

Life in Ancient Rome
Life in a Wild West Show
Life in Charles Dickens's England
Life in Communist Russia
Life in Genghis Khan's Mongolia
Life in the Amazon Rain Forest
Life in the American Colonies
Life in the Elizabethan Theater
Life in the Hitler Youth
Life in the North During the Civil War
Life in the South During the Civil War
Life in the Warsaw Ghetto
Life in Tokyo
Life in War-Torn Bosnia
Life of a Medieval Knight
Life of a Nazi Soldier
Life of a Roman Slave
Life of a Roman Soldier
Life of a Slave on a Southern Plantation
Life on Alcatraz
Life on a Medieval Pilgrimage
Life on an African Slave Ship
Life on an Everest Expedition
Life on Ellis Island
Life on the American Frontier
Life on the Oregon Trail
Life on the Pony Express
Life on the Underground Railroad
Life Under the Jim Crow Laws

THE WAY
PEOPLE
LIVE

Life in the Australian Outback

by
Jann Einfeld

LUCENT
BOOKS ®

THOMSON

GALE

San Diego • Detroit • New York • San Francisco • Cleveland • New Haven, Conn. • Waterville, Maine • London • Munich

On Cover: An Aborigine applies body paint on another, Arnhem Land, Northern Territory, Australia.

© 2003 by Lucent Books. Lucent Books is an imprint of The Gale Group, Inc., a division of Thomson Learning, Inc.

Lucent Books® and Thomson Learning™ are trademarks used herein under license.

For more information, contact
Lucent Books
27500 Drake Rd.
Farmington Hills, MI 48331-3535
Or you can visit our Internet site at http://www.gale.com

LIBRARY OF CONGRESS CATALOGING-IN-PUBLICATION DATA

Einfeld, Jann.
    Life in the Australian Outback / by Jann Einfeld.
        p. cm. — (The way people live)
Includes bibliographical references and index.
    ISBN 1-59018-014-3 (hardback : alk. paper)
    1. Australia—Social life and customs—Juvenile literature. 2. Australia—Juvenile literature. [1. Australia.] I. Title. II. Series.
    DU107 .E37 2003
    994—dc21

2001007504

Printed in the United States of America

Contents

Discovering the Humanity in Us All

Books in The Way People Live series focus on groups of people in a wide variety of circumstances, settings, and time periods. Some books focus on different cultural groups, others, on people in a particular historical time period, while others cover people involved in a specific event. Each book emphasizes the daily routines, personal and historical struggles, and achievements of people from all walks of life.

To really understand any culture, it is necessary to strip the mind of the common notions we hold about groups of people. These stereotypes are the archenemies of learning. It does not even matter whether the stereotypes are positive or negative; they are confining and tight. Removing them is a challenge that's not easily met, as anyone who has ever tried it will admit. Ideas that do not fit into the templates we create are unwelcome visitors—ones we would prefer remain quietly in a corner or forgotten room.

The cowboy of the Old West is a good example of such confining roles. The cowboy was courageous, yet soft-spoken. His time (it is always a he, in our template) was spent alternatively saving a rancher's daughter from certain death on a runaway stagecoach, or shooting it out with rustlers. At times, of course, he was likely to get a little crazy in town after a trail drive, but for the most part, he was the epitome of inner strength. It is disconcerting to find out that the cowboy is human, even a bit childish. Can it really be true that cowboys would line up to help the cook on the trail drive grind coffee, just hoping he would give them a little stick of peppermint candy that came with the coffee shipment? The idea of tough cowboys vying with one another to help "Coosie" (as they called their cooks) for a bit of candy seems silly and out of place.

So is the vision of Eskimos playing video games and watching MTV, living in prefab housing in the Arctic. It just does not fit with what "Eskimo" means. We are far more comfortable with snow igloos and whale blubber, harpoons and kayaks.

Although the cultures dealt with in Lucent's The Way People Live series are often historically and socially well known, the emphasis is on the personal aspects of life. Groups of people, while unquestionably affected by their politics and their governmental structures, are more than those institutions. How do people in a particular time and place educate their children? What do they eat? And how do they build their houses? What kinds of work do they do? What kinds of games do they enjoy? The answers to these questions bring these cultures to life. People's lives are revealed in the particulars and only by knowing the particulars can we understand these cultures' will to survive and their moments of weakness and greatness.

This is not to say that understanding politics does not help to understand a culture. There is no question that the Warsaw ghetto, for example, was a culture that was brought about by the politics and social ideas of Adolf

Hitler and the Third Reich. But the Jews who were crowded together in the ghetto cannot be understood by the Reich's politics. Their life was a day-to-day battle for existence, and the creativity and methods they used to prolong their lives is a vital story of human perseverance that would be denied by focusing only on the institutions of Hitler's Germany. Knowing that children as young as five or six outwitted Nazi guards on a daily basis, that Jewish policemen helped the Germans control the ghetto, that children attended secret schools in the ghetto and even earned diplomas—these are the things that reveal the fabric of life, that can inspire, intrigue, and amaze.

Books in The Way People Live series allow both the casual reader and the student to see humans as victims, heroes, and onlookers. And although humans act in ways that can fill us with feelings of sorrow and revulsion, it is important to remember that "hero," "predator," and "victim" are dangerous terms. Heaping undue pity or praise on people reduces them to objects, and strips them of their humanity.

Seeing the Jews of Warsaw only as victims is to deny their humanity. Seeing them only as they appear in surviving photos, staring at the camera with infinite sadness, is limiting, both to them and to those who want to understand them. To an object of pity, the only appropriate response becomes "Those poor creatures!" and that reduces both the quality of their struggle and the depth of their despair. No one is served by such two-dimensional views of people and their cultures.

With this in mind, The Way People Live series strives to flesh out the traditional, two-dimensional views of people in various cultures and historical circumstances. Using a wide variety of primary quotations—the words not only of the politicians and government leaders, but of the real people whose lives are being examined—each book in the series attempts to show an honest and complete picture of a culture removed from our own by time or space.

By examining cultures in this way, the reader will notice not only the glaring differences from his or her own culture, but also will be struck by the similarities. For indeed, people share common needs—warmth, good company, stability, and affirmation from others. Ultimately, seeing how people really live, or have lived, can only enrich our understanding of ourselves.

Different People, Different Lives

A ustralia's Outback is vast. It covers more than three-quarters of the continent of Australia—2.2 million square miles of land—and is about the size of the forty-eight mainland U.S. states. Geographically, the Outback branches out in all directions from the heart of Australia, and it is cradled to the east and west by the highly populated eastern and southwestern coastal regions.

The Outback is generally characterized as dry, harsh, unyielding, and even hostile. Popular images of the Outback include red dirt tracks merging into endless vistas of open country, scorching temperatures, whirling dust storms, and devastating drought. These images seem fitting because Australia is the oldest, driest, flattest, and most infertile of all inhabited continents on Earth. However, such descriptions of the Outback are too confining; it is in fact a land of great diversity.

Land of Many Contrasts

The Outback comprises not only the scorched and barren lands of central Australia and some of the driest inhabited deserts on Earth but also rich tropical rain forests, flood- and cyclone-prone coastal areas, and dense scrubland and bushland. Paul Myers, publisher of *Outback Magazine*, says:

> The Outback is the Red Centre and the Simpson Desert, the Barkly Tableland and the Top End, the Gulf of Carpentaria

and Cape York, the Nullarbor Plain and the Pilbara, the Channel Country and the Strzelecki Track and all the regions, towns, stations and settlements in between. But it's also there on the Great Divide, and in southwest Tasmania, along rivers and on the coast, in rainforests, in the north, south, east and west; anywhere, indeed, that's remote, off-the-beaten-track, different and quintessentially Australian.[1]

If remoteness is a major feature of Outback country, so is scarcity of people. Less than 10 percent of Australia's 19 million people live in the Outback. And the small number of inhabitants are as varied as the landscape.

Diverse Lives

The people of the Australian Outback are a mixture of cultures, traditions, lifestyles, and adaptations. Aborigines, who have inhabited the continent for thousands of years, live in townships, on settlements, and on ancestral lands, where they practice ancient cultural traditions with modern adaptations. Cattle station owners maneuver helicopters in pursuit of cattle roaming freely across stations spanning thousands of miles of Outback country. Nomadic sheep shearers move from station to station, doing the backbreaking work of removing the wool from sheep's backs. Greek, Italian, Croatian, and Timorese workers haul cattle, sheep, and wool thousands of miles across the continent in road trains, the largest trucks in the world. A multicultural array of miners populate Outback opal fields, drawn to the glitter of precious stones and by their dreams of striking it rich. Tour guides, entertainers, civil servants, doctors, and teachers live in Outback towns, providing a welcome respite for travelers and residents from the isolation of Outback living. Australian author Thomas Keneally describes the people who make up the Northern Territory:

Southwest of [the town of] Katherine, horsemen eat breakfast with a helicopter pilot who will work above their heads all day, driving cattle out of their hides [skins] in the long grass and mulga [dry zone bush] scrub. . . . At Timber Creek the manager of a cattle station drives up to the pub, a [nineteen-foot] crocodile [that killed his prize stallion], shot and trussed, in the back of his truck. . . . At Mongrel Downs beyond the Tanami Desert, a girl of nine receives by two-way

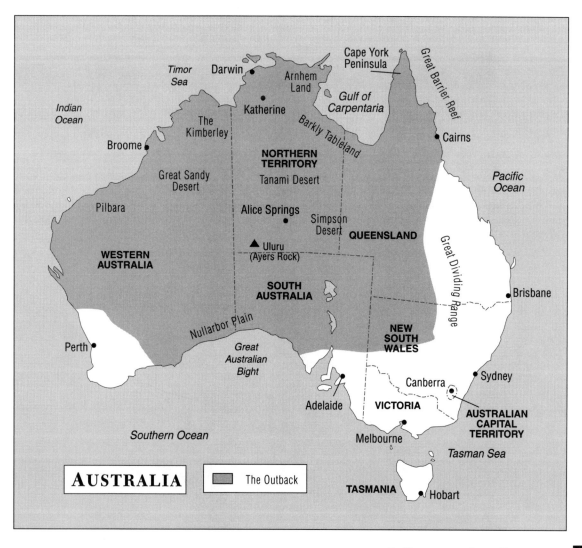

radio an English lesson from the School of the Air in Alice Springs, [440 miles] away along a red dust track. Above the Barkly Tablelands a flying doctor makes a final approach to a dirt airstrip marked with forty-four gallon drums painted white. By the strip lies a twenty-two-year-old stockman whose ankle has been crushed by a Land-Rover which rolled while he was chasing a wild bull. At Docker River the [Aboriginal] elders waylay six adolescents and take them away through Livingstone Pass for a three-week-long initiation ceremony as ordained by the heroes and ancestors of the Dreamtime [the time of creation according to Aboriginal beliefs].[2]

Spirit of the People

Despite differences in their lives and ways of seeing the world, people of Australia's Outback share certain traits. Endurance is foremost. With a determination to survive and thrive under conditions of extraordinary hardship, Outback people endure devastating droughts,

An Aboriginal man starts a fire with sticks in the Australian Outback.

Herding sheep on an Outback station.

watch entire herds drown in massive floodwaters, and see their homes consumed by raging brush fires. Yet they return and rebuild their lives. After a prolonged drought in Western Australia, Pinnacles Sheep Station owned by Helen McKinnon's family got two years of rainfall in four days. Nearly all their stock drowned, and the family home was ruined, but they carried on. Helen recalls:

> We were very composed about it. We'd just killed a beast and were sitting down to a piece of roast beef. The water just flowed across the floor. It was ten inches deep in the house for two nights and we all slept on the back of a truck. . . . Eventually the civil defense landed and took us to the local town. . . . It took six months to clean the house and we lost three thousand ewes and the young sheep just drowned.[3]

Outback people also overcome obstacles imposed by vast distances and social and cultural isolation. From finding food and water in barren deserts to the delivery of first-rate health and education services, Outback people demonstrate ingenuity in dealing with their environment. This ingenuity is fueled by their deep attachment to the haunting beauty and power of the landscape. Says one Outback resident, "Our love for . . . the land we live in and which lives in us is as powerful as it is eternal."[4] By its very untamable nature, the Outback commands respect, even reverence. And the people of Australia's Outback, each in their own unique way, are as unconquerable as the land itself.

An Ancient People

Australia's indigenous people, the Aborigines, were the first inhabitants of the Australian Outback. They have a unique cultural heritage that is based on an intimate relationship with nature and the land on which they live. This heritage includes rich and complex spiritual beliefs and traditional laws, which guide the people in all aspects of their daily lives. Ronald Berndt, who has studied Aboriginal culture, says, "Aboriginal religion is intimately associated with everyday living, with relations between the sexes, with the natural environment and with food-collecting and hunting. . . . Their religion is a total way of life."[5]

This way of life has proved strong and resilient through more than two hundred years of exposure to Western influences. Today, Aboriginal people in the Outback live in a variety of settings—in large towns, in Aboriginal townships, on rural settlements, and on traditional lands. The different communities choose to adapt to modern influences in varying degrees. As a rule, for instance, groups who live in the larger townships closer to main highways use more modern technology in their everyday lives than those in smaller groups in remote locations. However, no matter where they live, their spiritual beliefs and traditional laws continue to provide the framework for their daily lives. Aboriginal writer Irene Watson says:

Traditional culture is not only being maintained in remote northern Aboriginal communities. In . . . cities and rural towns—languages are spoken, kinship obligations are met, traditional customs are observed and Aboriginal people are caring for their country. . . . Our people are affirming the . . . continuing relevance of [our spiritual beliefs] to our lives today.[6]

The Dreamtime

Aboriginal spiritual beliefs are based on the mythology of the Dreamtime. The Aborigines believe that the Dreamtime was a time, long ago, when the Australian continent was transformed from an empty and featureless plain by the activities of a large number of ancestral beings. These beings were humanlike but could assume animal form. Gifted with superhuman powers, they came out of the earth and down from the sky to walk on the land. They shaped its rocks, rivers, mountains, deserts, and forests. Winding creekbeds were created by the movement of an ancestral snake; gaps between the hills were opened by a blow from the stone ax of a fighting lizard man, and large boulders were once the eggs of an emu ancestor.

The spirit ancestors also created all the people, animals, and plants that were to live in the country. Dreamtime legends and stories tell of their travels and adventures. When the ancestors completed their work, they went back into the earth. Aborigines believe they are descendants of one of these spirit ancestors. The particular spirit ancestor from which each Aborigine is descended is known as a totem. Totems act like an emblem or badge to unite a group of people who believe they have common ancestry.

Social Organization

Aboriginal spiritual beliefs guide the people to live in communities of clans, or groups made up of several families who share a common totem. A totem might be a snake, caterpillar, kangaroo, or even a rainbow. When Jen Gibson, who studies the lives of Aborigines, met with a group of women in Oodnadatta in South Australia, one woman explained how their common ancestry united all the male and female members born in the area. "We all

have in our body a birthmark of a snake's head. . . . I have my Dreamtime snakehead on my leg. We all have this little white patch, we all have this Dreamtime birthmark on us."[7]

Each ancestor is associated with a particular area of land and some sacred places, called Dreaming sites. Aboriginal people are responsible for maintaining their Dreaming sites, which might be a dry riverbed or group of rocks in a remote desert location. Maintaining a Dreaming site involves keeping it in the same condition as it was in the Dreamtime and ensuring that people do not disturb the site. Aboriginal people believe there can be serious consequences if Dreaming sites are desecrated. When Gibson visited a snake Dreaming site with the women of Oodnadatta, they

These rock paintings are Dreamtime figures linking the Aborigines to their ancestral spirits.

Aboriginal Land Rights

According to eighteenth-century international law, an imperial power like Great Britain could acquire any territory it wanted, provided the land was unoccupied. When the first British fleet arrived on Australian shores in 1788, they claimed that the land was an uninhabited desert. Because the Aboriginal people did not till the land or employ European agricultural practices, the British did not recognize that the indigenous people had any rights to the land. Thus the British declared Australia *terra nullius*, or land owned by no one. On this basis, white settlers moved into the continent, evicted the Aborigines, and used their hunting grounds for grazing and agriculture. This caused great hardship to the Aboriginal people, who believe their role as caretakers of their traditional lands is the very purpose of their existence.

Two hundred years later, Aboriginal activists challenged the concept of *terra nullius* in Australia's highest court. In 1992, after a ten-year court battle, judges ruled the British assumption had been false. The judges ruled that there was such a thing as native title, or the right of Aboriginal people to own land, which preceded European occupation of Australia. This decision had enormous symbolic as well as practical significance for the Aboriginal people. Symbolically, it showed respect for the Aborigines' ancient culture and way of life. In practical terms, large tracts of land were returned to Aboriginal people, who now own it legally. As a result, many Aborigines have chosen to return to the land of their ancestors, where they are free to practice their traditions and make their own decisions about how they wish to live.

European settlers herd their sheep through a chute.

An Australian Aborigine hammers a sign into the ground marking a sacred cater-pillar Dreaming site.

told her that the small rocks standing upright were the remnants of their snake ancestor and must not be touched or the number of dangerous snakes in the area would greatly increase. The responsibility for preserving these sacred sites is taken very seriously. Aboriginal writer Mudrooroo explains that "to destroy them is to destroy some of the earth energy and thus weaken all that live and breathe."[8]

Traditional Housing

In addition to determining where and with whom they should live, families draw upon religious legends and stories as a guide for how they should live. This includes their houses and how they use them. Most Aboriginal people in the Outback, like their ancestors, prefer to live, cook, and sleep outdoors. Whether in a traditional or a more modern setting, Aboriginal housing is very simple, and is used principally for shelter from extreme weather.

Traditional Aboriginal dwellings, which are still found in remote Outback regions, are simple structures made of sheets of bark propped up on a framework. The houses' design is based on a Dreamtime story in which the first bark hut was built by two legendary figures, the bush-nut man and his wife, for protection from the monsoon rains of the northern Outback.

If weather in an area is often severe, more substantive bark huts are built. These use more bark to protect the occupants from high winds and rest on raised platforms to escape floods. An Aboriginal woman recalls gathering supplies to build one of the larger huts:

> When these huts were built, it was very hard work. . . . We . . . went so many miles out bush to get all our barks, spent all day just collecting barks, making large fire to burn the barks to keep them firm and strong . . . flattened them on the ground and put weight of logs and stones

A bark hut in the Northern Territory abandoned by Aborigines was used as seasonal shelter.

on them, until the evening came. We all came home with great loads of barks on our heads and on our sides, hung down from the shoulder by a string or a belt. . . . We had no other way to carry all the load. . . . So you see, it was very hard to start to build a house of bush barks.[9]

In many Aboriginal Outback communities today, modern technology has made hut building and life in general easier. Aboriginal families in townships and rural settlements often live in simply constructed one-room houses made of timber, corrugated iron, and concrete. Sometimes there is a water supply and electricity to power televisions, refrigerators, and washing machines. Communications technology includes radio receivers and telephones driven by solar power. However, in most cases, these modern facilities have been adapted to the Aboriginal way of life. For example, Aboriginal houses are still simple structures

used principally in bad weather, and communication technology is often used to contact groups to arrange traditional ceremonies.

Finding Food and Water

Ancestral laws also lay down the rules for hunting and gathering food and finding water. In general, Aborigines do not cultivate crops or raise livestock. Instead, they depend on the earth in its natural state to provide for their needs. Although today, many Aborigines in urban areas and on larger settlements get food from grocery stores, knowledge of special trails along which food and water can be found in the Outback is highly valued. And an intimate understanding of the character and habits of prey is still passed down through the generations.

In some cases, the information is related through song. These songs, known as Songlines, act as mental maps of the landscape. Aborigines believe these songs originated thousands of years ago and were created by their spirit ancestors. Many of the songs have hundreds of verses, yet every song must be memorized exactly. A song's tune reflects the shape of the land: long passages of low notes connote an open flat plain; high and low notes suggest undulating country. Knowing these songs enables Aboriginal people to find their way around the Outback and tells them where to find game or water. In emergencies, such

knowledge can be critical. Writer W.E. Harney, who lived among the Aboriginal people, describes one such emergency:

Once, when I was crossing a dry part of the north-western desert, my truck broke down. I had some water, but not enough to keep my native passengers and myself alive if our engine fault proved to be serious.

Life in Two Worlds

Some Aborigines choose to leave their ancestral homes for life in towns. When they do, they often take on attributes of a European lifestyle, like a Western diet and clothing. However, they continue to take great pride in knowing the traditional laws and ways of their people. In the following extract from his autobiography *I the Aborigine*, Douglas Lockwood, who works as a physician on an Aboriginal settlement, describes his satisfaction in being able to hunt using traditional weapons:

"One weekend I took my family on a hunting walkabout. I threw off my clothes, changed into a narga [loin cloth], picked up spears and woomera [spear thrower] and walked towards the edge of the clearing which defined the boundary of the settlement. . . . I had not hunted for a year or more. My food had been served on plates, and I was accustomed to eating with a knife and fork. It was sophisticated food sold by butchers and bakers, tinned and packed in foil, aseptic and often frozen. Although I ate and enjoyed it, I was always conscious that something was missing: the tang of game freshly killed and cooked in a camp-fire, the deep satisfaction of living by my wits as my forefathers had, and I had, along the Roper [River]. . . .

As I moved across the clearing with [my wife] Hannah and the children behind me I was conscious of spontaneous laughter. Bush people who had been coming to me for treatment were hysterical with delight and astonishment.

'Look at the doctor! . . .' they yelled. 'H-a-a-ah!' . . .

Their ridicule was incessant and insufferable. They were saying in effect: 'what does this silver-tail [privileged person] know about hunting? He wouldn't know upwind from downwind, a wallaby track from a goanna's [large lizard], the sharp end of the spear from the blunt end!'

That evening I walked back through the clearing in silence so complete it was complimentary. Across my shoulders and around my neck I wore the badge of rank of a Master Hunter: a dead wallaby. . . . At the clinic the next morning I reappeared in clean clothes and began treating the daily parade of sick and injured as though nothing had happened. They continued to address me as 'doctor,' but in their voices I detected the inflections of a deeper respect than they had previously shown me."

It was sixty miles to the nearest water, but an old Aborigine told us not to worry, for, although he had never been in that locality, he knew the "map-chant" [Songline] of the area.

So, while we [the other Aborigines and myself] worked on the engine, he sang his chant. A long while he chanted, till he came to the landmarks that stood around us, and in the cool of the evening, he made us walk with him as he chanted. We obeyed.

His song now was of a low hill before us, and from it, the story went, we would come upon the markers of stone which pointed to water. We climbed the hill and saw the cairn of stone laid down by an early Aboriginal explorer, and beside it was a line of rocks which pointed to a low depression of limestone. To it we went, and there, under a covering of logs and grasses, was a limestone crevice that led into a small pool of crystal clear water.[10]

Knowing how to find water is the key to survival in the vast Outback deserts, and Aborigines can find water where there is no appearance of moisture. They know that secret stores of water can be found in the roots and branches of desert oak trees. Sometimes they lie on the ground and listen for water underneath the earth. They have highly tuned senses that can even smell and feel water in the breeze. They also know that the water-holding frog, the cyclorana, burrows beneath the earth with an abdomen full of water waiting for the next heavy rains to fall. During severe droughts, Aborigines dig these frogs from their burrows and squeeze the moisture from their bellies.

Aboriginal Languages

When Europeans arrived on Australia's shores in 1788, there were between six hundred and seven hundred Aboriginal tribes living in Australia who spoke about 250 different languages. Many of the languages were distinct and did not permit different tribes to communicate with each other. For example, Aborigines living on opposite sides of present-day Sydney Harbor could not understand each other. However, scholars believe that originally all these languages were part of one language family that dates back thousands of years. This accounts for some words that occur everywhere across the continent—for example, *jina* (foot) and *mala* (hand).

Most Aboriginal languages have about ten thousand words. Many of those words reflect the close relationship Aborigines have with the land. For example, the language of the Western Desert Pintupi tribe has eighteen words for "hole." The large number of words delineating different types of animal holes reflects the Aborigines' intricate understanding of the natural world.

After prolonged contact with Europeans, many Aboriginal languages have been lost. For many years, Aboriginal people were encouraged to learn English and forbidden to speak their native languages in the presence of Europeans. As a result, only about twenty or thirty Aboriginal languages are in use today.

A hole in the earth provides a clue to a water source for the Aborigines in the arid Outback.

Aboriginal expertise on animal behavior extends well beyond desert frogs. An intimate understanding of how animals think and act enables Aborigines to devise tricks to track and snare their game. They might use an animal's sense of smell, habits, or curiosity to catch it. Kangaroos grazing on windy days, for example, will not catch scent of a hunter who smears his body with mud and ochre and approaches into the headwind. An inquisitive emu can be diverted by an unusual object laid in its path. On sighting an emu, hunters might lie on the ground and kick their legs in the air. As the emu moves close to look at this strange sight, hunters jump up and spear him. Australian historian Geoffrey Blainey says that Aborigines' use of mimicry, copying animal sounds, is also effective:

> A skilful [skillful] click of the tongue decoys crabs from holes in the mud of the mangrove swamps; a snake-like hiss can drive a bandicoot [large ratlike mammal] from a hollow log and an imitation of a hawk often halts a fleeing goanna [large lizard] so that he stiffens and stands still, becoming an easy target for the huntsman.[11]

Hunting Implements

The sophistication of the hunters' techniques stands in contrast to the simplicity of their traditional hunting implements. Spears with wooden points or stone heads are the most common traditional weapon of Aboriginal hunters. Most of these spears range from five to nine feet long and weigh four or five pounds. Hunters often use a woomera, or spear-thrower, to enhance their spear-throwing accuracy. This wooden instrument, about two and a half feet long, is used as a launching pad. It operates as an extension of the hunter's arm. Labumore, an Aboriginal woman, says woomeras "help to send the spear as far as the man wants it to go, also to direct the straight

The spear, common to Aboriginal hunters, is an accurate weapon, especially with a woomera attached.

shot to strike any object that he aims for. Without no woomeras to go with the spear, you never can feed yourself."[12]

Boomerangs are also part of the traditional armory used to hunt game. Boomerangs are curved wooden instruments, some of which are designed to return to the thrower. Returning boomerangs are used most often for killing birds. Heavy nonreturning boomerangs are lethal weapons in the hands of a skilled marksman and are used for large game, such as emus and kangaroos.

Hunting implements have multiple uses. For example, spears can be used to settle conflicts between clan members, and the woomera for digging holes or as a mixing bowl for preparing paints used in religious rituals. Boomerangs double as musical instruments in ceremonies and have religious and symbolic significance. Mudrooroo says: "The boomerang is more than a bent throwing stick that returns. . . . It was first fashioned from the tree between heaven and earth; it symbolizes the rainbow and thus the rainbow snake; and the bend is

the connection between opposites, between heaven and earth, between Dreamtime and ceremony, the past and the present."[13]

Today, in more modern communities, these traditional implements have been replaced or modified. Rifles and guns are used instead of spears and woomeras, and spears may be tipped with blades of metal rather than stone. However, in remote reaches of the Outback, traditional hunting weapons are still used. No matter where Aborigines live, they take great pride in being able to use these hunting implements proficiently.

Bush Tucker

The food Aborigines hunt is also part of their rich spiritual life. They believe each food was created by the ancestral beings. According to legends, some foods are even ancestral spirits changed into another form: The honey ants of Papunya in Central Australia, for instance, are considered by Aborigines in that area to be part of the honey-ant ancestor. Religious beliefs also dictate certain rules about what food can and cannot be eaten. For example, certain people have special links with certain foods that are their totems. These people are often forbidden to kill or eat their totems except during special religious ceremonies.

The food Aborigines hunt and gather is called bush tucker. This includes many animals and plants. Aborigines eat wallabies, wild horses, lizards, snakes, bugs, ants, termites, anteaters, fish, worms, crocodiles, and even wild camels. Witchetty grubs, wormlike creatures that live in the roots of certain acacia bushes, are high in protein and fat and are eaten raw. Aborigines also eat many different types of fruit, nuts, and seeds. In the Cape York region in Northern Australia, 141 species of plants are known to yield food to Aborigines. This includes 73 fruits, 46 roots, 19 kinds of nuts, and 11 varieties of green leaves.

In some communities, primarily townships and settlements, foods like flour, sugar, and canned goods have largely replaced bush tucker. However, many Aboriginal groups living on traditional lands still maintain a traditional diet. Rosemary van den Berg, specialist on bush foods, says, "[Aborigines still] practice traditional food-gathering . . . and continue to hunt kangaroo and emu . . . and catch snakes, lizards and goannas . . . and gather and forage for delicacies from the bush. . . . The only difference now is that these food sources [may be supplemented by] items from the supermarket."[14]

Rituals for Ensuring the Food Supply

Hunting and gathering activities are closely interwoven with harvesting practices and religious rituals designed to ensure that the food supply is plentiful. For example, women who collect yams always put back some of the yam in the ground. They believe this will placate the yam spirit, who might grow angry if all the yams were harvested. Aboriginal women in Cape York in northern Queensland tell their children: "When you dig up yam, you must all the time leave [a] little bit . . . of that yam in the ground. . . . If [you] dig it all out, then that food spirit will get real angry and won't let any more yam grow in that place."[15]

Rituals called increase ceremonies are also important to ensuring the food supply. Only men who have been initiated into the ways of the tribe can participate in these ceremonies, which are conducted early in the spring all over the Outback. Robert Tonkinson, who has lived with Aborigines in Central Australia, describes an increase ceremony for emu eggs: "The group [of Aboriginal men] . . . approach the [sacred site of the emu ancestor] and the men clean all around it. One of the men then steps forward and addresses the emu spirits thus: 'We want emu eggs. Make plenty. Give us

A close-up view of bush tucker, an ochre from which Aboriginal meals are made.

lots. We want some for eating, some for emus—for meat! Keep them coming!'"[16]

Preparing the Evening Meal

Religious laws also govern the way Aborigines prepare, cook, and eat traditional foods. In general these laws serve practical purposes. Many plant foods, for instance, are indigestible or poisonous if they are not properly treated. Certain species of nuts need to be leached in water to remove toxins, and the outer coverings of grass seeds must be removed to make them suitable for eating.

Women are responsible for this job and use traditional methods to accomplish it. To remove grass seed coverings, for example, Aboriginal women dig a hole in the ground near a tree and pour in the grain. Holding onto the tree, they stand on the grain and grind the husks away by rotating their feet from side to side. The wind then blows away the unwanted chaff, and the grass seeds are ground with water into a paste, which when baked is called damper.

Most Aboriginal people also prefer to use traditional means to prepare meat. Although some families on modern settlements have stoves in their houses, Aborigines, consistent with the ways of their ancestors, like to cook their meat in underground pits. Labumore describes how her family cooks and serves a wallaby:

> We dig a long deep covermarie hole [a hole in the ground with a fire at the base, covered by bark]. When the fire dies out

Aboriginal women use wind currents to help separate the chaff from acacia seeds.

The Australian Dingo

Dingoes are wild Australian dogs. They are important to Aborigines because they assist with the hunt and accompany women in their search for food. Dingoes also keep Aborigines warm on cold nights. In fact, Aborigines describe nighttime temperatures as a one-dog, two-dog, or three-dog night. In *Linkletter Down Under*, American comedian Art Linkletter describes his experiences in owning a sheep station in Western Australia. In the following extract, he says Aborigines are very protective of their domesticated dingoes and treat them like members of the family:

"Aborigines consider dingoes to be semisacred, perhaps the incarnation of spirits, and are very protective of them. An Aborigine will not kill a dingo puppy nor tell a white man where a wild dingo den is located. If a dingo becomes vicious in an Aborigine camp, he will be 'tried' by a council and if found guilty, staked out on a beach at low tide and left there to be drowned by the incoming water. In this way the Aborigine is absolved of personal guilt in the dingo's death. An Aborigine will say the dog was well the last time he saw him; it must have been the tide that killed him.

Thus the dingo occupies a secure place in the social structure of the Aborigines.

They are addressed by their owners, generally women, as if they were members of the family. And if the dingo misbehaves—for instance, bites—he is treated in kind: the offended person does not beat the dog; he bites him. Aboriginal punishment is based, quite literally, on an eye for an eye."

A dingo surveys the territory around him.

we put the wallaby in, then put bark over the wallaby, then put little bit of coal over the bark, then bury it up with sand. When the old tribes [elders] think it's cooked enough they undo the covermarie, with another bark for a table, and place the wallaby on the bark. No matter how much campers are there, the wallaby meat is divided into each family.[17]

Social Life

Aborigines usually share their food, whether plant or animal, with their clan. Ancestral laws dictate that sharing is essential to promote harmonious living. Thus, personal greed or hoarding is frowned upon. One Aboriginal woman says: "My people [are] very kind hearted people, never selfish. They . . . [have]

to share whatever they [have], even the last bit of food [they've] got. They never [keep] it for themselves, but [are] always willing to share and give away."[18]

Sharing food is not the only code of behavior outlined in religious law. Many social rules and taboos, established by the ancestors, must be observed. For example, people with the same totem cannot intermarry; men cannot speak to their mothers-in-law; when they reach puberty, brothers and sisters must not speak directly to each other; and when a brother marries, his sister must treat her sister-in-law in the same way. An Aboriginal woman gives an example: "Say, for instance, I walk past my brother and sister-in-law at their camp. I must not get too close. I must walk ten . . . yard[s] away from their camp. I'm not even allowed to speak to my sister-in-law. That too is how we show our love and respect to her, because she got married to him."[19]

Through this system, every Aboriginal knows how he or she is expected to behave with other members of the family and the community. These rules give Aborigines a strong sense of security. It makes them feel they are linked to all other Aboriginal people and can call upon them if they need help. Robert Tonkinson says: "People talk with satisfaction about the good feelings that come from being surrounded by so many others who are 'one family,' 'one country' and 'one people' with them and from whom nurturance and support can be sought."[20]

Aboriginal life is not all rules and directives, however. Aborigines enjoy spending time together and having fun. There is normally ample leisure time for sleeping, playing with small children, and one of the favorite pastimes, storytelling around an evening campfire. Carol Morse Perkins, an American who has lived and traveled with Aborigines in the Northern Territory, recounts a typical evening:

Evening was a wonderful time in camp. The work was done for another day. The food had been gathered, and everyone returned safely home. Eating the delicious fish, they told each other of the day's adventures. Then as darkness closed in about them, they drew closer to the fire and talked of Dream Time. They told each other of their ancestors and their legends of how the world was made. Frogs were croaking in the distance and it reminded one of the old men, called Koolootaroo, of the [Aboriginal] myth of the frog woman named Quork Quork and her family. He began [to tell the story].[21]

Corroborees

After storytelling, Aboriginal women clear away the food and put the children to bed. Select male elders meet to discuss tribal business. These elders make up the tribal council, and they are responsible for planning ceremonies that are an integral part of Aboriginal daily life. Says Aboriginal spokesman Manadawuy Yunupingu, "Our ceremonial activity often lasts for weeks at a time and is practiced by thousands of people in the bush on a day-to-day basis."[22]

Traditional ceremonies are called corroborees. Corroborees are held at night and enact stories of the Dreamtime ancestors through celebrations of song and dance. The male performers usually dress up to resemble an animal, a plant, or an event from a particular clan's Dreamtime story. For example, the main performer of the emu clan has a headdress like the long neck of an emu.

In corroborees, men's costumes include feathers glued to their bodies with blood and intricate patterns painted on with red and yellow ochre. All these patterns have symbolic meaning that relate to a Dreamtime story. For example, circles represent frogs, red string represents thunder, and black strings symbolize rain falling from the sky.

Performers move like the animals they represent, reenacting the movements of their ancestors. Baldwin Spencer, who studied the Aranda tribes in Central Australia, explains, "They [the Aranda performers] are supposed to represent the ancestors and to behave as they did and be decorated as they were in the Dreamtime. They may prance around, quiver like the wind, wriggle like a worm, leap like a kangaroo or snap like a crocodile."[23]

Initiation Ceremonies

Some corroborees are secret ceremonies that only men and the boys ready to be initiated or welcomed as men into the tribe can attend. During these corroborees, or initiation ceremonies, boys who have reached puberty learn the secrets of the tribe from the older men. They learn their ancestral laws and the sacred places of their ancestors through song, story, and dance.

Initiation ceremonies are a time of physical ordeals, which can include circumcision, knocking out a boy's two front teeth, and

Aboriginal men dance at a corroboree honoring their Dreamtime ancestors.

Young boys await their initiation ceremony welcoming them as men into the tribe.

requiring him to endure a day lying in the broiling sun without food or water. These trials test a young man's strength and ensure that he can withstand hunger, fear, and pain to establish whether he can be entrusted with tribal secrets. If a boy breaks under the ordeals, he must try again when he is a year older. When a boy passes these tests, his tribe believes he has died and been reborn as a man. After he has passed the ordeals of initiation, a boy's father says something special to his son. One Aboriginal father took his son's hand and said:

> Today you are learning the truth for the first time. . . . All the [tribes'] sacred [laws] are entrusted to you for safekeeping. Protect them, guard the home of your fathers, honor the traditions of your people. We still have many things to tell you. . . . They are all your own heritage: we have only kept them in trust for

you. Now we are getting old, we pass them on to you. . . . Keep them secret until you are growing old and weak.[24]

Violation of Traditional Laws

Most Aboriginal boys accept the responsibility given to them during initiation ceremonies. They know that revealing sacred information to the uninitiated is a major violation of tribal law and transgressors will be punished. Aboriginal people generally think such punishment is necessary because they believe natural calamities like floods or droughts result from the ancestors' anger when laws are broken. As this affects the welfare of the whole tribe, penalties must be harsh. One Aboriginal woman says, "My tribe's laws were so strict. You could not fool around with any of their laws. You interfere wrongly with . . . tribal life, you have your punishment."[25]

The most extreme punishment prescribed for serious offenses like unlawful marriage or permitting the desecration of sacred sites is called "pointing the bone." Most Aboriginals believe in the death-dealing potency of the bone. They fear that once a tribal elder with the powers has pointed the bone at them, they will quickly become ill and die. Pointing the bone is accompanied by a special chant that Aboriginal people believe extracts the victim's spirit from his body and kills him. The chant has many variations. The following is one example:

Kill Goggle Eye [term for the head of the bone], kill Goggle Eye, make him dead-fellow;

Pull away his fat, make his bonefellow [a skeleton];

Shut him up throat, shut him up throat;

Break him out heart, break him out heart;

Kill him deadfellow, kill him deadfellow;

S'pose him eat fish, poison him with it;

S'pose he eat bird, poison him with it.[26]

These punishments are just one way Aboriginal laws continue to provide the framework for an Aborigine's daily life. Whether hunting for food, participating in corroborees, or relating with each other, Aborigines in the Australian Outback have preserved their unique traditions. These traditions give the people a strong sense of identity and connection with the land. "It is the law we have lived since time began," says Yunupingu, "and through this process, our identity is one with mother earth."[27]

Cattle Mustering and Sheep Shearing

Many people in the Australian Outback make their living raising sheep and cattle on stations sprinkled through the interior of the country. Work on these stations is hard and requires great skill and physical endurance. However, it is also exciting and rarely fails to captivate those involved. One Outback station owner from the Northern Territory describes the atmosphere during the main cattle station activity called mustering, or herding the cattle:

> The thrill of the pace and chase of the muster [herding] never fails to stir the most seasoned ringers [stockmen or cowboys]. Ready to ride, they focus on the plan and the paddock: each moment of each muster is charged with concentration, commonsense and variation. Excitement pulses through blue veins as they make their way across the beckoning plains.[28]

Outback Stations

Outback stations are large areas of land where families live and work raising sheep and cattle. Sheep are grown for wool and cattle for beef, both of which Australia exports all over the world. Sheep stations are located primarily in the southern areas of the Outback, in New South Wales, South Australia, and the southern area of Western Australia. The more hardy cattle are better adapted to the drier areas of the northern Outback. Some families own and run several stations and raise both sheep and cattle. For example, the Field family in Outback New South Wales owns 120,000 sheep and 3,000 cattle on five stations with a total land area of 27,000 acres. However, most families own just one station and specialize in either sheep or cattle.

Because vegetation is sparse in the Outback, stations require large areas of land to provide adequate feed for their animals. Hence sheep and cattle stations are vast. Sheep stations average fifteen thousand acres and cattle stations twenty-five thousand acres, but many are much larger. In fact, Australia's Outback is home to some of the largest cattle stations in the world. Cattle roam thousands of acres of backcountry over areas that rival the size of whole European countries. For example, Alexandria Station in the Northern Territory, at 2.3 million acres, is larger than Belgium.

Work on the stations revolves around the once- or twice-yearly herding of the animals. This activity is governed by the weather, and each station, large or small, sets up a work routine that relates to the seasons. For example, during the wet-season months of January and February in the north, roads and station tracks become impassable and paddocks waterlogged, making it impossible to handle cattle. So in the northern Outback, work to prepare for rounding up the cattle usually begins in March.

Mustering Cattle

In the Outback, rounding up cattle is called mustering. Mustering is done to select the animals in the best condition for selling and to brand and castrate new calves into steers, which make tastier beef. Station owners sell their cattle for beef in Australia or for export. In some cases, live animals are sent overseas for slaughter or for breeding.

In most cases, cattle are mustered twice a year, summer (December through February) and winter (June through August). The larger muster is in winter when it is cooler for the men and the animals. The group of people who muster the cattle is called a mustering team. This team usually consists of six or seven people, some of whom will fly aircraft; others ride horses or motorbikes. A team of three to four bull catchers, specialists in removing unruly wild bulls, and a cook are also part of the mustering team. When cattle numbers are large and the animals spread out over a vast area, mustering teams might be out on the far reaches of the station for four to six months. However, on most stations mustering lasts four to six weeks.

Mustering Operations

The first task of the mustering team is to catch and break, or train, a good fleet of stock horses to be used for the muster. These horses may be wild horses, or horses that stations regularly use for mustering and are set free at the end of each season. Station horses that have been set free are usually very spirited and need to be retrained by the stockmen to make them suitable for riding.

Horses are broken in by stockmen, called ringers. Each ringer will be given anywhere from four to six horses to work and look after. To break in the horses, the ringers first lunge them on long lead ropes around the paddock. Then they get the horses used to having the

The Cattle King

Innovative approaches to managing Outback stations trace their roots to people like Sir Sidney Kidman (1857–1935), one of the most famous men in Australian pastoral history. During the late nineteenth century, when vast expanses of Outback Australia were being settled, there was no infrastructure like roads or water holes. Moving cattle across great distances to markets was very difficult. Kidman came up with the idea of "chains" of stations along strategic routes. These chains were a series of stations where stockmen and cattle stopped and rested, allowing the gradual movement of stock from inland to coastal markets.

Born in 1857 in Adelaide in South Australia, Kidman ran away from home at the age of thirteen. He headed to northwestern New South Wales, where he found work on Outback cattle stations. Here he became an expert bushman and stockman. At twenty-one he inherited four hundred pounds (about eight hundred dollars), which he used to buy cattle and horses, and later gold mines. Gradually he built up a portfolio of landholdings on which he set up his chains, eventually owning or controlling almost sixty-six thousand square miles of land. Today the Kidman family still owns and operates some of the largest cattle stations in the outback.

weight of a saddle on their backs, before finally mounting them. When the horses are used to being handled, ringers shoe them to protect their hooves from the stony Outback country.

In the last ten years, some station owners have replaced many of their mustering horses with motorbikes. These owners find motorbikes easier to transport to the mustering sites, and believe the bikes can move the cattle more quickly and more effectively than horses. However, even though fewer horses are used today, they still play an important role. One Northern Territory station owner says, "Horses are an important part of life on [our station] despite the increasing mechanization of station activities."[29]

With horses broken in and ready for the muster, small planes are sent on reconnaissance missions to locate the cattle. Herds of cattle, called mobs, roam across hundreds of miles of Outback country. Mobs can be anywhere from a couple of hundred to several thousand head. Flying about four thousand feet above the countryside, pilots follow the cattle and study their routines, particularly the direction of cattle movements to water holes. (Large groups of cattle gathered at a water hole will be relatively easy to catch.) These pilots are experts in the habits of cattle and in the layout of the countryside. Thus, once they get the information they need, pilots can effectively direct the ground crew operations. One pilot's wife said, "Ashley [the pilot] understands where the stock [animals] will be in certain seasonal conditions and the weather conditions of the day. He knows how fast they'll run and for how long, and how to direct the [mustering] ground crew in the most efficient manner."[30]

Setting Up Camp

With information on cattle movements, pilots then look for the best place to set up camp.

A mustering helicopter will fly high above mobs of cattle to study their movements.

Drought

Severe drought is an ever-present threat in the Outback, where rainfall averages only four to nine inches per year. In *Icing on the Damper: Life Story of a Family in the Outback*, Marie Mahood, who has lived on remote cattle stations in the Outback all her life, recalls her family's experience during a severe drought in the 1980s:

"I honestly don't know how [my husband] Joe stuck it out with the continual breakdowns of vital equipment, the ever present stink of dead cattle and the wispy grass and dying trees in the bare paddocks. Eventually he opened up all the paddock gates to let the cattle forage at will, so the strongest would survive because they could walk further to graze and would not be constrained by fences. He bought what hay was available to hand feed the horses and a nucleus of the breeding herd and it was pitiful to see those pathetic cows gallop frantically towards the vehicle when I helped to throw off the hay bales at the weekend. We had to ration them, just enough to keep them alive, because the hay was so hard to get, with ten times more needed in the district than was available.

'Buck up, Hon,' said Joe with a light touch on my shoulder, when he found me howling one day over the death of a cow, one I'd petted and fed by hand and looked for particularly each weekend because she'd been a hand-raised poddy [motherless] calf a few years before. It seemed the last straw to me.

I was instantly appalled at my weakness. It was I who should have been supporting Joe, not making things harder. He was the one who had to do the thankless and repetitive work, to make the hard decisions and face the dreadful task almost daily of shooting those poor beasts that were never going to struggle to their feet again. He faced the stark drought almost every day without respite, alone for most of the time, and I had five days of every week with . . . the distraction of a [teaching] job that took my mind off the misery of the drought. I never howled again."

This will be a location that is as close to the main mob as possible but is also accessible to the large trucks, called road trains, which pick up the cattle to take them to market. Once the spot has been chosen, teams of horses, men, motorbikes, and cattle dogs are loaded into large trailers and brought to the campsite.

When the men arrive, they set up camp. First they unload the supply truck, which includes the cook's supplies and utensils, as well as generators used to provide power to refrigerate fresh and frozen food. Then they unload the sleeping bags, or swags. Swags are weatherproof bedrolls that open into thick rubber mattresses and blankets. They have heavy waterproof flaps that can be pulled across the occupant in case of rain. Ringers sleep in their swags directly under the stars with no other protective covering.

After setting up camp, the ringers' first task is to erect portable mustering yards. These yards are necessary when the herd is very spread out or a long way from the main station buildings. Portable yards resemble the permanent yards found at the stations. They include separate paddocks for branding and castration, and loading areas for moving the cattle onto the road trains. Mustering yards usually take one or two days to build. The yards have one set of gates, and from these gates, an enormous

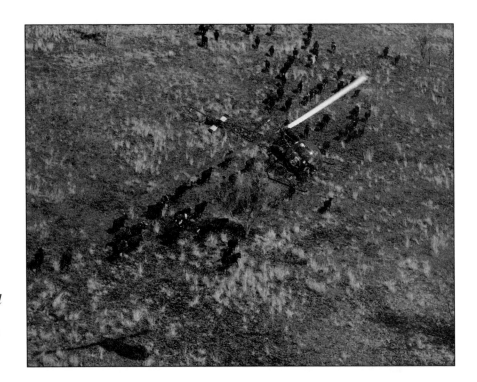

Cattle are followed and controlled by air before they are mustered on the ground.

hessian (a strong, coarse cloth) funnel is constructed with an opening about sixteen hundred feet across. This funnel helps channel large mobs of cattle into the yards.

Mustering Begins

Mustering cattle is a carefully coordinated effort. The teams in the air and on the ground work together to gather and gently move the mob in the direction of the mustering yards. The muster begins when the planes or helicopters find the herd at water holes. Flying close to the ground, the aircraft begin to round up the main mob and move the herd. Stockmen on horseback ride at the back of the mob, motorbikes work at the sides, and cattle dogs round up the strays. Station manager Terry McCosker, from Lawn Hill Station in Outback Queensland, describes his mustering teams' operations:

We wait for the chopper to get the cattle under some sort of control before bringing in the ground musterers. The wild cattle run like blazes through the timber, but the chopper is able to stay with them and keep the mob together. We let them run in a rough direction towards where they want to go, and when they start to calm down a bit we bring in the men on horseback.[31]

The work is hard, the days are long, and the risks are significant. When several aircraft operate in a confined space, they may collide, or the herds can stampede and scatter all over the countryside. Writer Thomas Keneally describes one mustering operation he observed in Western Australia:

The noise of aircraft, the protest of the mob, the roaring and whistling and whip-cracking of the stockmen create a tremendous rage of sound, and the dust is prodigious [everywhere]. The helicopters and the cessna [plane] are now very low. It is accepted aviation practice that fixed wing aircraft and choppers should not operate close to each other. But here are three aircraft, all as low as [sixteen feet], all having to concentrate not only on the cattle but on their distance from the ground and from each other, helicopters hovering, the aircraft banking, circling, returning within the same dusty and restricted volume of sky. By the time the cattle are near the funnel, you have not eaten since 5 A.M., the sun is high, your mouth is full of red dust. And you do not know whether it will all work.[32]

On the ground, none of the riders talks much while mustering. As temperatures rise to ninety or one hundred degrees, flies come out in swarms, attacking eyes, nostrils, and open mouths. By the end of the day, the ringers' eyes, ears, and mouths are also filled with red dust from the whirling helicopters and the animals' hooves. In these tough conditions, the skill of the ground crew is no less impressive than that of the pilots. Ringer Colin Stone writes:

Twelve men mounted and riding out of camp, spurs and whips at the ready, was a sight to be remembered. Throughout the day I could hear the constant cracking of whips, shouting and cursing. I could see

Bush Poets

Outback stockmen and sheep drovers have a long tradition of reciting poetry at night around the campfire. One of the most popular poems, written by Australian bush poet Banjo Patterson, is "Clancy of the Overflow." The poem is about a man trying to get in touch with his friend Clancy, a stockman who travels from station to station and is difficult to reach. The following extract from this poem appears in *The Collected Verse of A.B. Patterson*.

"I had written him [Clancy] a letter which I had, for want of better Knowledge, sent to where I met him down the Lachlan [River], years ago; He was shearing when I knew him, so I sent a letter to him, Just 'on spec' [speculating], addressed as follows: 'Clancy of the Overflow.'

And an answer came directed in a writing unexpected,

(And I think the same was written with a thumbnail dipped in tar);
'Twas his shearing mate who wrote it, and verbatim I will quote it:
'Clancy's gone to Queensland droving, and we don't know where he are.'
In my wild erratic frenzy visions came to me of Clancy
Gone a-droving 'down the Cooper' [River] where the western drovers go;
As the stock are slowly stringing, Clancy rides behind them singing,
For the drover's life has pleasures that the townsfolk never know.
And the bush hath friends to meet him, and their kindly voices greet him
In the murmur of the breezes and the river on its bars [ridges],
And he sees the vision splendid of the sunlit plains extended,
And at night the wondrous glory of the everlasting stars."

the dust rising from the pounding of many hoofs, as horses and cattle dodged in and out of the scrub. . . . There were men riding at full gallop chasing a runaway bullock [steer], blocking and turning its direction back toward the main mob. Horses becoming over-excited, sometimes rearing or bucking and unseating their riders. It was a very exciting time of dust and sweat and curses of frustration, until the sun dipped low and we had mustered and drafted as many cattle as we could during the day.[33]

Bull Catchers

Working alongside the men on horseback are highly specialized teams of men who catch wild bulls. Removal of these bulls from the herd is necessary to keep the other animals quiet and to prevent interbreeding with the purebred cattle. Even with modern bull-catching vehicles, this is one of the most dangerous jobs on a cattle station. Teams of motorbikes, helicopters, and special vehicles designed to chase, tip over, and tie bulls are used. Journalist Rachel Smith describes the efforts of one bull-catching team, brothers Danny, Damien, and Cameron Parker from Outback Queensland:

Soon the chopper is overhead and cattle are racing through the scrub. . . . They [the brothers] tail [follow] the bull [on motorbikes] through wattle [dry-zone brush], over stump holes and darting in and out of trees until it shows signs of exhaustion and slows. Then the men are off, running, the bikes still rolling unmanned, and the brothers are wheeling on the tails of the bull and dodging the

Mounted ground crews, called ringers, bring the cattle together in a tight muster.

Road train drivers have challenging jobs driving enormous trucks to transport sheep, cattle, and produce thousands of miles across harsh Outback country. Jeff Gilbert began driving trucks across the Nullarbor Plain in South Australia when he was sixteen years old. In the following extract from *We Live in Australia*, edited by Rennie Ellis, Gilbert describes his work:

"These days I mostly do the Adelaide-to-Darwin run. The journey is about [two thousand miles] right through the center of Australia, most of it is on the one road. . . . Sometimes in the Northern Territory I have three trailers on and this can make the whole rig about [165 feet] long. I think they're the longest trucks operating anywhere in the world. I do the trip all through the year and the road conditions can go from one extreme to the other. In the dry season it's hard with corrugations and dust. In the wet you can get three inches of rain in a couple of days and I've known blokes [men] to be stuck in the mud for a week. We always carry extra food rations just in case.

I usually do a trip every two weeks, average speed [28 mph]. I take a lot of equipment up to the Peko gold and copper mines at Tenant Creek, north of Alice, and also to the uranium mine at Jabiru. And I take beer to Alice Springs. . . . I use [1,200 gallons] of diesel fuel a trip. The tractor takes [470 gallons]. Some of the trailers have belly tanks under the chassis and each of these holds [240 gallons]. So I might be carrying [950 gallons] of fuel at the start of the trip.

The round trip usually takes seven days if all goes well. On average you get two or three punctures a trip. When I've got two trailers on I'm looking after forty-two wheels plus I've got eight spare tires. . . . I check the tires every two hours. . . .

I've got air conditioning, about forty cassette tapes to play and there's a CB radio so if anyone's around you can have a bit of a yak [talk]. If there's accidents or emergencies you can hook up to the Flying Doctor radio. . . . I see a lot of wildlife—dingoes, kangaroos all the time, wild horses and cattle, emus. Further north there's wild pigs, camels, donkeys, and up top there's the buffalo. . . . Yeah, it can be a tough life, but I like it."

horns. Damien flicks a hat in the face of a bull to distract it from its charge and, as it tosses its horns dangerously close, Cameron swings on the tail and the bull hits the dust with its full weight.[34]

With the bull on the ground, the bull catchers strap its front and back legs. They saw off the tips of the horns to make the animal less dangerous to handle. Bull catchers then use a winch to haul the animals up a ramp onto a truck that will take them to the larger trucks that transport them to the station yards. Here the bulls spend about a week adjusting to captivity, learning to eat hay and drink from troughs, before being reloaded onto trucks bound for live export boats at one of Australia's major shipping ports.

Loading the Cattle

Ringers bring the rest of the cattle to the portable yards. There, some of the herd will be branded, castrated, and set free. Others, those that are to be sent to market, will be loaded onto road trains. At 168 feet, road trains are the longest trucks in the world. Most have at least three trailers with six decks that can accommodate 144 steers each. Drivers back the vehicles up to the portable mustering yards, and the cattle are loaded quickly and efficiently for their long ride to the slaughterhouse. Writer Fiona Lake describes the loading operation at Brunette Downs, one of the largest stations in the Northern Territory: "The trucks wait patiently, cabs wobbling gently as the [880-pound] steers stomp up the ramps. A total of 576 steers are loaded onto four trucks . . . at a rate of fifteen minutes a truck—just an hour to load the lot. Nine hours later the cattle have a 24-hour spell at Mt Isa [in Queensland] before the final twenty hours to . . . market."[35]

With the cattle safely loaded, mustering teams pack up camp and return home. The bull catchers and some of the ringers will move on to another station and another muster. Ringers employed by the station will resume their regular station work, which includes maintaining water holes, fences, and station equipment.

Sheep Country

Although smaller than cattle stations, sheep stations are also huge. Coronation Hill Station in Western Australia, at half a million acres with twenty-five thousand sheep, is the biggest sheep station on record. However, most family sheep stations might have five thousand to eight thousand sheep over an area of fifteen thousand acres.

Work on sheep stations revolves around shearing season. In the drier areas of the southern Outback, the timing of the sheep shearing is a matter of personal preference.

A road train scatters dust as it speeds toward its destination, the slaughterhouse.

Station owners consider the climate, the season, and the condition of the sheep. On Commonwealth Hill in New South Wales, for example, shearing is planned for January. Sheep are then relieved of their wool in the hottest months and can grow new coats to protect them from winter frosts in May.

During sheep shearing season, sheep shearers, called sundowners, are hired to remove the wool from the sheep's backs. They are a hardy breed of highly skilled workers who lead a nomadic life, moving from station to station as work becomes available. They are strong, fit, and have a reputation for being big drinkers with keen senses of humor. Their arrival at the sheep stations is the high point of the year. American comedian Art Linkletter, who owns a station in Western Australia, says, "The visiting sundowners bring an air of excitement to the place. These nomad shearers tend to be a rough, tough, blasphemous breed . . . a rough and ready element of Australian society which does a very difficult job with fierce independence."[36]

A ringer maintains surveillance of the cattle range with his canine companion.

Teamwork

Shearers usually work as part of a team for a contractor who lines up jobs at different stations. Contractors are hired by the sheep station managers to supply the shearing team. Teams are made up of five or six shearers, a "rouseabout" who picks up the wool and sweeps the floor, a wool classifier who separates the wool into different grades, and the cook, who accompanies the teams to every job to prepare their meals.

Once the team is assembled, the contractor sends a man in advance to the station to check the machinery. He checks and oils the electric shears, sharpens the cutters, tests the power supply, and makes sure the equipment is in top condition for the shearers. This job is an important one, because the efficiency of a shearer depends as much on his tools as on his skill.

When the equipment has been inspected, the next step is to muster the sheep and bring them to pens outside the shearing shed. Planes, helicopters, and motorbikes with two-way radios are used for this task. At Reola Station, one of the largest sheep operations in the Outback, a dozen stock workers muster the sheep using motorbikes, four-wheel-drive vehicles, and helicopters. The team drives sheep into the pens from 980,000 acres of grazing land. Even on smaller sheep stations, much of this equipment—particularly light planes and motorbikes with two-way radios in the helmets—is standard for mustering sheep.

In the Shearing Shed

Sheep that have been mustered are placed in pens outside the shed in preparation for shearing. Shearing is done in four two-hour increments, from 7:30 to 9:30, 10:00 to noon, 1:00 to 3:00, and 3:30 to 5:30, with two thirty-minute breaks for "smoko" (morning and afternoon tea) and an hour for lunch. The work requires great concentration and is very taxing on shearers' backs, so some shearers wear a harness for support. These harnesses are suspended from the roof of the shed and hold the shearer just below his chest. Veteran shearer Darrell Taylor says, "I've been wearing one for about 12 years. They don't look very strong but there's just enough to take the weight off my back."[37]

Conditions inside the shed are also trying. Shearer Oliver Vidgen recalls one of his tougher days: "The heat was like an oven, the shed was full of these big panting wethers [castrated rams] and you could reach up and touch the tin roof and burn your fingers on it. When we went back in to the huts [sleeping quarters] . . . it was still 115 degrees at 5:30 P.M."[38]

The Shearing Begins

At 7:29 A.M., the station manager switches on the motors, and the hum of the shears fills the shed. In accordance with strict labor union laws, the shearers do not start a minute before schedule and wait with anticipation for the clock to say 7:30 A.M. Journalist Matthew Cawood describes the atmosphere in the shed as work begins:

> It's 7:29 A.M. and the atmosphere in the shed is taut with nervous tension. Shearers study the penned sheep or fine tune their hand pieces. One is doing

stretching exercises. The minute hand on the clock hanging from a nail creeps imperceptibly around, until it reaches the perpendicular. There's a dry shriek from belts overhead. The overhead gear that drives the hand pieces has kicked into action. Wheels begin spinning. One after the other the shearers straighten up and wade into the pool of woolly backs in their catching pens, each hauling a big sheep onto the board. One by one the hand pieces start buzzing like manic metallic crickets until the air is full of their chatter. In a few seconds the shed is roaring with noise and bustle.[39]

After bringing a sheep onto the floor, the shearer quickly flips it over on its back and holds it upright between his knees. The goal is to sheer the fleece off in one large piece, which makes it easier to handle and so it can be sold for more money. On average, shearers clip a sheep in three to five minutes; most shear 70 to 100 sheep per day. Some do even more. Professional shearer Darrell "Farris" Taylor, for example, shears about 120 to 130 sheep a day.

The skill of the shearers often attracts the admiration of spectators. Jill Ker Conway, who grew up on a sheep station in New South Wales, recalls: "I never tired of watching the throbbing bustle of the woolshed operating at full speed. . . . Everyone's movements were so stylized that they might have been the work of a choreographer. . . . Bodies bent over the sheep, arms sweeping over the sides of the animal in long graceful strokes to the floor, the shearers looked like participants in a rite."[40]

However, even the most experienced shearers routinely nick or cut the sheep's skin with their shears. Sometimes blades run over a wrinkle of skin or sheep wriggle or jerk unexpectedly. Writer Margaret Rau describes how this happens:

Now and then a shearer may make a nick when the cutter runs over a wrinkle. . . . Sometimes the shears run into sand and dirt in the wool and become blunted. Then instead of clipping the shears start pulling. This makes the sheep kick and squirm into the cutter on top of the comb, causing a deep gash in the flesh. When this happens the shearer has to take time out to stitch up the wound with the needle and thread handy on a shelf at his side.[41]

Dipping the Sheep

These wounds must be treated with disinfectant to avoid insect infestations and infection. Without this precaution, large black blowflies lay their eggs in cuts in the skin. This can cause blood poisoning, a condition that will weaken or even kill the sheep.

The process of applying the disinfectant is called dipping. The reason is that until the latter part of the twentieth century, sheep were literally dipped into a tank that contained disinfectant. Today, however, herds of sheep are driven into cylindrical tanks and sprayed by a shower of disinfectant. Linkletter describes the scene: "While huddled in a round galvanized tin spray pen, sixty sheep at a time are sprayed from overhead with this strong liquid. The sheep protest loudly while undergoing this indignity."[42]

As they exit the pen, the sheep are lethargic from breathing the insecticide. However, they quickly recover and, relieved of up to

Sundowners quickly and diligently shear the wool from the sheep on a station in Victoria.

The Dog Fence Man

Australia's three-thousand-mile Dog Fence is one of the longest manufactured structures in the world. Its purpose is to stop vicious and predatory dingoes in the northern part of the country from reaching sheep in the south. In the following excerpt from "The Dog Fence Man," published in the October/November 2000 issue of *Outback Magazine*, journalist Liz Davis describes the life of John Norwood, whose job has been to maintain about 220 miles of fence for the last twenty years. It is an unusual and solitary lifestyle, but one that he loves.

"John Norwood sought the contract to maintain his section of fence in 1980 and has never wanted another job since. 'I always wanted to be a cowboy,' he admits carefully, 'I just can't stay at home all the time, I like to be out there.' Out there is John's stretch of fence. Every [two weeks] he covers [two hundred miles] from remote Fowler's Bay on the west coast of South Australia to Lake Everard in the Gawler Ranges, making repairs, checking for holes under or through the wire, camping out overnight and then moving on the next day. 'It takes about a week to cover it properly,' he explains, 'but camping out is the best. I don't think I've camped twice in the same place since I started. . . . I like the isolation . . . there's no one looking over your shoulder, it's just you and your job out in the bush.'

A sign explains the expansive boundaries of the dog fence.

twelve pounds of wool and dirt, are set free in Outback country to resume grazing.

Experts Sort the Wool

Inside the shed, once the sheep is shorn, shearers send the animal out an exit door. As the shorn animal exits on a shute, the shearer yells, "Wool away!" and the rouseabout rushes in to gather up the fleece. Rouseabouts are often considered inferior by the shearers and given a hard time because they do the lowly job of picking up the wool. Georgina Faulkner recalls, "Rousies are called dung beetles at first. . . . You learn to laugh and tell them to lay off."[43] However, both managers and shearers value good rouseabouts because their work requires skill and great physical endurance. Writer Selina Baxter describes the work done by one rouseabout from New Zealand:

> All day she watches keenly so that she will be instantly where she is most needed, keeping the board clean around each shearer, whisking the pieces away, bundling up the shorn fleeces, tidying up the bins of wool. . . . All day, she is bending, picking up, walking quickly up to the classer [classifier] and, with expert thrust [forceful push] of the shoulders and flick of arms, throwing the bundled fleece out onto the wool table, so that it falls gently and magnificently down to be skirted [trimmed] and classed.[44]

Once the wool has been collected, classifiers sort the fleece into different grades according to its whiteness, fineness, length, and strength. The whiter, finer, and larger fleeces are more valuable and will be separated from the poorer grades. If the feed has been variable during the season, meaning that the sheep have eaten well at times and poorly at others, the fleece and its grading will reflect this. Breaks in the quality of the wool indicate where the food was more or less nutritious, and the lack of uniformity will adversely affect its grading. Once the wool has been classed, it is put in a wool press and pressed into bales. About 250 wool bales weighing four hundred pounds each are then loaded onto waiting road trains to be transported to major shipping ports for export.

"Toughness, Tenacity and Endurance"

Wool classifiers, shearers, ringers, and bull catchers are highly skilled personnel whose work on Outback stations requires great physical endurance. Advances in technology—the use of planes, helicopters, and motorbikes for mustering; road trains; mechanized shears; and many other time- and labor-saving devices—have revolutionized Outback station operations. However, the seasons, the harsh and unpredictable weather, and the vast distances remain constant.

The characteristics of the people—hard work, physical endurance, and the ability to withstand heavy losses during tough times—also stay constant. One station owner says: "Although cattle management and lifestyle have changed dramatically, it is still [hundreds of miles] to town and a long way between watering points for cattle. . . . Despite the [technological] revolution, toughness, tenacity and endurance in man and beast are still essential today."[45]

At Home on the Station

Strong, self-sufficient families form the backbone of Outback life. The strength of families comes from their reliance on each other and a shared commitment to their life on the land. Family members work together, have fun together, and depend on each other to solve problems that arise. The distance from towns and other people and the hardships of daily life make this dependence on their own abilities essential.

The McFarlanes from Oxley Sheep Station in Outback New South Wales are a good example. After devastating losses caused by drought, the conversion of their river to mud with an infestation of carp, and low wool prices, the McFarlane family came up with innovative solutions to their problems. They implemented conservation measures and grew enough native vegetation to feed their six thousand sheep. Two new businesses, one producing fertilizer made from carp and the other selling saltbush-fed mutton directly to consumers as a specialty item, have increased station profits. As a result, the McFarlanes believe they can deal with whatever difficulties arise. Bob MacFarlane echoes the views of many Outback families when he says, "We have faith in the future of agriculture and the ability of our family to work together through any problems thrown at us."[46]

Station home and family life revolves around the homestead, a collection of buildings on the land where station families live and work. Homesteads vary in size according to the number of people who live there. In some cases a family of two adults and two children will be the only permanent station residents. However, on most stations this is not the case. There are usually workers who live in separate quarters near the family home.

Homestead Communities

The number of staff on family stations generally depends on how good the season has been. During good years when rainfall has produced adequate feed and beef and wool yields are expected to be strong, stations hire more staff. Helen McKinnon from Pinnacles Station in Western Australia says, "It's great having a good season and being able to afford staff. Seasonal conditions really dictate how easy things will be. . . . [After a good year] we employ a full-time gardener, several jackeroos [young stockmen in training], a governess and a girl to help run the house."[47]

Some homesteads are much larger than Pinnacles Station and have a permanent workforce of twenty or more people. For example, Killarney Station in the Northern Territory has more than sixty people living and working together. This includes stockmen, bookkeepers, mechanics, and cooks. Some of them are single, but others are married and live with their wives and children.

In addition to the permanent workforce, other workers come to live at the homestead during the mustering or shearing season. At mustering time at Lawn Hill Station in

Outback Dust Storm

Dust storms can last for days in the Outback. They often come with no warning, and residents have little choice but to stay indoors and ride it out. Usually the animals suffer the most. In the following extract from her autobiography, *The Road from Coorain*, Jill Ker Conway describes what it was like when dust storms came to her family's sheep station in Outback New South Wales:

"One sweltering afternoon in late March . . . glancing toward the west, I saw a terrifying sight. A vast boiling cloud was mounting in the sky, black and sulfurous yellow at the heart, varying shades of ocher red at the edges. Where I stood the air was utterly still, but the writhing cloud was approaching silently and with great speed. Suddenly I noticed that there were no birds to be seen or heard. All had taken shelter. I called my mother. We watched helplessly. Always one for action, she turned swiftly, went in doors, and began to close windows. Outside I collected the buckets, rakes, shovels, and other implements that could blow away or smash a window if hurled against one by the boiling wind. Within the hour, my father arrived home. He and my mother sat on the back step, not in their usual restful contemplation, but silenced instead by dread.

A dust storm usually lasts days, blotting out the sun, launching banshee winds day and night. It is dangerous to stray far from shelter, because the sand and grit lodge in one's eyes, and a visibility often reduced to a few feet can make one completely disoriented. Animals which become exhausted and lie down are often sanded over and smothered. There is nothing anyone can do but stay inside, waiting for the calm after the storm. Inside it is stifling. Every window must be closed against the dust, which seeps relentlessly through the slightest crack. Meals are gritty and sleep elusive. Rising in the morning, one sees a perfect outline of one's body, an afterimage of white where the dust has not collected on the sheets. . . .

It was three days before we could venture out, days of almost unbearable tension. . . . It was always a miracle to me that animals could endure so much. As we checked the property, there were dead sheep in every paddock to be sure, but fewer than I'd feared. My spirits began to rise and I kept telling my father that the damage was not too bad. 'That was only the first storm,' he said bleakly. He had seen it all before and knew . . . [there was more] . . . to come."

Dust storms on the Outback keep humans indoors and send animals in search of cover.

Queensland, for instance, sixteen stockmen, a mechanic, two cooks, a bookkeeper, and four professional bull catchers join the station family to become part of the homestead community.

These homestead communities form highly self-sufficient units. Station personnel do their own building and plumbing, fix vehicles, rebuild engines, and tend to sick animals. Most station families live almost entirely on homegrown food. Sheep and cattle supply meat, and many homesteads raise chickens for eggs and poultry and grow their own produce. David, Kerry, and Judith Bowthorn, from Bowthorn Cattle Station in the Northern Territory, are a brother-and-sister team who are a good example of a self-sufficient station family. Author John Andersen says:

> The homestead garden grows all the station's fruit and vegetable needs. . . . Towards the end of each year, when the heat kills all but the hardiest plants, Kerry starts making preserves. She bottles enough vegetables to keep them going until the garden once again begins to bear after the wet season [December–February]. . . . David is considered to be by many people in the district a genius with ma-

chinery. Give him a [wrench] and a screwdriver and he'll get the biggest wreck in the world going. . . . Judith has taught herself saddlery and makes all the saddles and harness equipment used on the station. The two sisters and brother, each in their own way, have skills which are injected into the property. Combined, these skills represent a formidable talent.[48]

The Homestead

The design of the homesteads reflects this same self-sufficient spirit. Because they are many miles from towns, homesteads are not supplied with water, electricity, or phone cables. Thus, they are designed with this in mind. Solar-, wind-, or diesel-driven generators supply electricity. Water comes from underground sources and is usually pumped aboveground by windmills or generator-driven motors. Telephones are powered by satellite dishes or solar energy.

With these utilities in place, the design of a typical Outback homestead will include four or more buildings, storage sheds, large storage tanks, a satellite dish, a radio antenna, muster-

This portrait of an Aboriginal farm owner from the Northern Territory, shows independence and grit.

Setting up life on Outback sheep and cattle stations can be hard. Sometimes new station owners do not appreciate how difficult their lives will be or how much persistence and perseverance will be required to cope with the inevitable setbacks involved in living in the Outback. In the following extract from Melissa McCord's book *Outback Women*, Marie Bronson, who is from an Outback station in Western Australia, tells her story:

"We decided to get Hooley Station. The owners had dumped sheep at the homestead to make it look good. After we arranged finance and came back up here, the sheep had got into the house and couldn't get out. They were on their last legs and the house was full of manure. It took ages and ages to clean up. There were dead sheep in the well. There was no garden at all, no yards, not even a [wrench] on the place. We've built it all up from scratch. . . .

I bought paint for the house and painted the outside. I got wallpaper for the bedrooms and the lounge, but the rains ruined the paper. I had carpet but the house got flooded and it got wrecked. . . . But I've never let anything get the better of me. I want to make the house look nice and [my husband] Snow has his heart set on it too. I get put back to square one, but I don't let it get me down. You persevere. Wouldn't be here if you didn't."

ing yards, and on some stations, an airstrip. Lyn Litchfield, from Wilpoorinna Sheep Station in the South Australian Outback, describes her homestead: "The homestead is the house and the sheds and the buildings, and there are shearers' quarters, and we've got an overseer's cottage although we don't have an overseer—we use that for the schoolroom. And there's the implement shed, and the generator shed, and the stables, and the chook [chicken] yard, and the garden."[49]

At the center of every homestead area is the family home. Houses are made from stone, brick, or corrugated iron. They are large and functional, and their design reflects the climate, isolation, and self-sufficient lifestyle of the families who live in them. Doors and windows promote drafts to help occupants survive stifling hot summers. Screens help protect occupants from the swarms of large, black blowflies, which appear in the summer months. Windows and doors are well sealed to minimize red dust buildup when dust storms envelop the property, and large storage rooms equipped with extra refrigerators are essential given the harsh and unpredictable weather conditions.

The Mail and Supplies

Most supplies for Outback stations are delivered by mail carriers who travel in four-wheel-drive vehicles or by air. Routes for Outback mail carriers are vast and usually cover hundreds of miles. In Outback Queensland, Cape York Air representatives boast they have the world's longest mail run. For the Cape York Air "mail man," whose day starts at 7:30 A.M. and ends at 4:30 P.M., his longest route covers almost a thousand miles and the shortest covers five hundred miles. At least thirty-six take-offs and landings occur between destinations, and trips can last for barely five minutes to well over an hour between stations.

Mail carriers are very important because they save Outback residents tremendous

Outback Washing

In the absence of washing machines, some Outback families have developed an unusual approach to doing the laundry. They place all their dirty clothes in a watertight drum along with detergent and cold water, and then put the drum in the back of their four-wheel-drive vehicle. They then go about their usual station business with the wash swishing and swirling around in the back of their vehicle. After several days traveling over bumpy dirt roads—the rougher the better—the clothes have been thoroughly washed. Some residents say this method achieves a better result than using a washing machine.

amounts of time. Stations are often situated hundreds of miles from the nearest town or post office over rough dirt roads. These conditions make it nearly impossible for residents to get mail and supplies on their own. Sharon Oldfield at Cowarie Station in Western Australia, for example, would have to drive six hours each way over poorly paved roads to pick up her mail in Maree, the closest town to her station.

Outback mail carriers understand this and know how important their deliveries can be to isolated families. For this reason, carriers are usually dedicated and hardworking individuals. One manager of nineteen postal workers who cover six thousand square miles in Outback Queensland says it takes a special breed of person to be an Outback mail carrier. "They've got to be the kind of person, who if

A Western Australia homestead such as this may be situated in an area hundreds of miles from a post office.

they're driving along and the road is blocked will detour [five hundred miles] to get the mail through to the person on the other side."[50]

Contact and Necessities

Mail carriers deliver a range of items essential to people's lives in the Outback. They bring food, school correspondence materials, spare parts, and medical supplies. A typical plane cargo list might include fruit, vegetables, groceries, tires, parts for an air conditioner, a microwave oven, newspapers, a box of medicines, and a couple of sun hats.

Many Outback people rely on the service for more than just mail and supplies, however. Mail carriers also bring much-needed social contact. During the rainy season in the north, mail crews might be the only visitors some residents have for weeks at a time. Given unreliable telephone reception during this season, sometimes mail carriers will be their only contact with the outside world. Thus, station families usually greet their mail carriers with great enthusiasm. When the mail carrier in North Queensland made it through during a break in a particularly long rain, Julie Hardaker and her family were thrilled. Ken, the mail carrier, relates their conversation: 'Was there something urgent you were waiting on?' I asked. 'Human contact,' Julie exclaimed. 'After days and days of rain and the kids spending 24 hours in the house, your patience wears thin. When all the creeks and rivers have joined up and you're cut off from the rest of Australia, it's so good to see another human being!'[51]

Knowing the mail carrier can sometimes help out in a medical emergency is also a comfort to Outback residents. "It is a great comfort to know that it is there in case we need transport urgently, perhaps for medical supplies or transport to the south,"[52] says Sharon Oldfield.

The RFDS

The distance from medical care is a valid concern because people on Outback homesteads might live hundreds of miles from a doctor or hospital. Roads and dry creek beds become impassable. And given the nature of the hard physical work station residents do, accidents happen easily. A stockman might fall from his horse or be injured by an angry

Outbreak Rescue

Receiving adequate medical care in the Outback requires the services of dedicated doctors from the Royal Flying Doctor Service (RFDS) in cooperation with residents. Rescues are often difficult because of the remote location of patients. In the following extract from "True Life Stories" on the RFDS website, RFDS doctor Balmain tells the story of an Outback rescue:

"It was a quiet Monday morning in the [RFDS] office, what a sentence! The billy [kettle] was being boiled for smoko [tea break] when the telephone rang. A stockman from the station [in Queensland] was mustering on his horse when the horse tripped and fell and rolled on the stockman. As it got up, it kicked him in the back. The man was instantly paralysed. Fortunately on that occasion there was another ringer with him and he was able to [call for] help.

A vehicle with an HF [high frequency] Radio in it was dispatched to the scene who then reported back to the station the stockman's condition and the station staff then contacted myself. Communicating directly with the people at the scene by HF Radio in the vehicle . . . my orders were to leave him absolutely as they had found him and not move anything. . . .

We departed Charleville [in south-central Queensland] for the station. On . . . arrival . . . we offloaded the necessary emergency equipment from our aeroplane into the station ute [truck] and drove to the homestead to take stock of the situation. We were told that the location of the accident was some two and a half hours driving away from the homestead over very rough Diamantina Channels [dry flood plains in western Queensland].

Fortunately a small two-seater mustering plane caught my eye, but I was told there was no room for any equipment in the helicopter. Helen [the nurse] agreed to come . . . in the ute with the equipment on board whilst I took a handful of diagnostic equipment in the helicopter and flew more rapidly out to the scene. . . . When I arrived at the scene and working with only the contents of one small bag, I . . . found . . . a 49 year old man with quadriplegia, unable to move any limbs at all because of his spinal injury. At that stage there was nothing I could do except wait until the utility arrived with our equipment in it some two and a bit hours later. . . . On arrival of the equipment, working in the heat, the dust and the flies, we transferred the patient, very gently from the ground onto a special spinal mattress. The trip over the Diamantina channels obviously took a lot longer than the outward trip for fear of causing further damage to his spine. Back at the station various tubes, pipes, masks and bags were placed appropriately and massive doses of the appropriate steroid was given intravenously. . . .

Contact was then made with the spinal injuries unit of a major Brisbane Hospital, who agreed to accept him. . . . The man is now back in full time employment."

bull. Heavy machinery might sever a finger or injure a child.

Until the 1920s, people in the Outback often died from illnesses and injuries for want of prompt medical attention or advice. Then in 1928 Reverend John Flynn, a minister of the Uniting Church, founded the Royal Flying Doctor Service (RFDS). The RFDS employs doctors and nurses who fly in to remote parts of the Outback to treat patients in serious condition. If needed, RFDS doctors arrange for patients to be airlifted to hospitals in towns or cities. Today the service operates from twenty bases throughout the Outback. It is a relief for Outback families to know that medical assistance is no more than two hours away in case of emergencies.

The job of the RFDS doctors involves challenges unknown to city physicians. Communicating with people over crackly radio receivers and providing instructions on how to administer injections, deliver babies, or handle a life-threatening stroke victim is not easy. Furthermore, many other difficulties cannot be foreseen. Outback doctor Jessica Richards, for example, says caring for patients in a small, noisy aircraft caused problems she had not anticipated when she began in the service:

Working in a small aircraft is difficult. You can't even use your stethoscope because you can't hear anything through it. That was the one thing that really shocked me when I started. So you have to use your clinical skills on the ground—you basically have to know everything you want to know before you start the engines; you've got to be able to face any emergency that might happen in flight.[53]

Treating People at Home

Most ailments do not require RFDS doctors to airlift patients to hospitals, however. Generally, residents are diagnosed and treated at home. Every Outback home is equipped with a special medical chart that numbers each body

Planes like this one bring RFDS doctors and nurses to Outback residents.

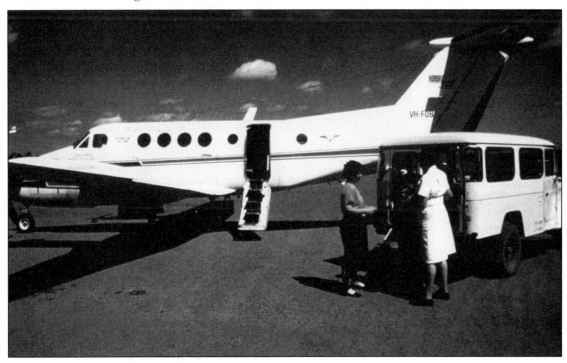

part. RFDS doctors or nurses ask patients over the telephone or radio to identify what hurts by the number on the chart. Medication is also numbered for easy reference. Lyn Litchfield from Wilpoorina Station explains: "When people are ill you can call up the Flying Doctor and he'll prescribe something. Every homestead's got a Flying Doctor medical chest, and each drug's got a sticker on it with a number, and he'll say it by number so people aren't confused with the names. Like he'll say on tray B give your child 5 ml three times a day of number 21. So it's all simplified."[54]

Sometimes treating people at home is not so simple, though. Outback families have to rely on each other to be able to comply with the instructions of the physician. This may involve difficult procedures and require immediate action. Marie Mahood, who lives on one of the most remote cattle stations in the Northern Territory, recalls her family's experience when her husband Joe's blood pressure soared after an allergic reaction to eating shrimp:

The doctor told [Mahood's daughter] Kim, that if the pulse rate had not dropped near to normal in five minutes she must give an injection of adrenalin straight into the heart muscle and explained how to do it and stood by as she [Kim] prepared the syringe.

"Now," said the Doctor, "time's up. Take his pulse again."

The rate had dropped considerably but was still very high. Joe, conscious but paralyzed marvelled at Kim's calm efficiency.

"We'll wait another five minutes and check again," said the Doctor.

The next reading was much lower and the danger past, although Joe was weak and shaky for some hours and his blood pressure did not return to normal for nearly a year. . . . Once again, we had good reason to say "Thank God for the Royal Flying Doctor Service!"[55]

Families and Family Roles

Family members depend on each other not only in medical emergencies but also in their everyday lives as part of a team. Husbands and wives form the nucleus of the family teams, and surviving in the harsh Outback conditions requires that they make a major commitment to the lifestyle and to each other. Thus, marriage in the Outback is highly valued and divorce is rare. For her book *Outback Women*, author Melissa McCord interviewed women living in stations all over Outback Australia. She concluded: "The isolation means that women have a more intense relationship with their men [than in the towns or cities]. . . . Frequently, it is a partnership between man and wife, a knowledge that they really need one another. Few men and women are openly affectionate, but I often sensed a strong bond—real *mateship* [deep friendship]."[56]

Historically, roles for husbands and wives in the Outback were fairly traditional. Usually, men managed the cattle or sheep operation, and women ran the home and family and schooled the children. However, this situation is changing as more women choose to become actively involved in the management of the station. Today daughters of station owners aspire to follow in their father's footsteps and manage the family station. Twenty-seven-year-old Alex Anning from Reedy Springs Station in North Queensland, for ex-

A female ringer manages her herd on horseback.

ample, is head stockman and plans to run her family's station one day.

Initially, women like Anning often encounter resistance from men when they step into nontraditional roles. Many ringers and stockmen have never had a female boss and are not used to taking orders from a woman. However, when women show they are competent, they usually earn the respect of the men. Anning says that stockmen accept her leadership if she proves she knows what she's doing: "The ringers [stockmen], mostly blokes [men], when it gets to the cattle side of things, they've got to realise I'll give the orders. . . . It might be a surprise when they first start, but they accept it. If you know what you're talking about it's fair enough [they're prepared to go along]."[57]

Horse-riding is a favorite pasttime of Outback children.

A Kid's Life

Like most Outback children, Anning learned about station work from early childhood. Outback children are relied upon to make a serious contribution. Their daily responsibilities might include checking fencing and water supplies on their motorbikes, shooting predatory dingoes, and feeding motherless calves. Most learn to drive a truck as soon as their feet can reach the pedals, so they can go for help if there is an accident.

Because they are given adult responsibilities, Outback children mature at a young age. Their training begins as a toddler. Terry Underwood, from a Northern Territory cattle station, says:

From infancy our little ones contributed to the development of our cattle station home during the crucial foundation years. Chubby fingers helped plant trees and lawn and keen eyes followed tracks and weather patterns. As they learned to speak on the two-way radio and change a tyre [tire] almost before they could walk, their childhood was, in a way, an apprenticeship. It was all about survival. It still is about survival.[58]

Sometimes the work is grueling. On cattle stations, helping adults brand cattle with red-hot irons and castrate them into steers is hot and difficult work. Work on sheep stations can be just as demanding. Jill Ker

Conway, who grew up on a sheep station in Outback New South Wales, for example, recalls how hard it was to apply disinfectant to sheep who had infestations of blowfly eggs in cuts made during shearing. She says:

> Dressing fly-blown sheep was hard, hot work because one had to round up the particular flock, get the sheepdogs to hold them, and then dive suddenly into the herd to tackle the one animal whose fleece needed attention. An agile child was better at doing the diving than an adult and in time I would learn to do a kind of flying tackle which would hold the animal, usually heavier than myself, until my father arrived with the hand shears and disinfectant.[59]

Life is not all work on the stations. Families enjoy spending time together and participate in a number of activities including horse-riding, picnics, barbecues, cricket, and swimming. However, the main social event is the picnic races, amateur horse races held all over the Outback, usually midyear when there is a lull in the station work.

For many Outback families, picnic races are their annual family vacation. The main horse races are held over two or three days, but some station families arrive up to ten days early to train their horses and set up camp. Stations owners bring their fastest horses to compete in the main race and in mini-rodeos. Rodeos feature bronco branding, calf roping, steer wrestling, and bareback broncing. At the races, parents and children also play games together, such as the three-legged race, and children take advantage of the opportunity to mingle with others their own age. In the evenings adults and children attend dances, and at night everyone camps out.

The Oak Park Races, which are held along the banks of the Copperfield River in Queensland in August, is one of the larger

Wanted: Minister on Patrol

Throughout the Outback, ministers from the Uniting Church, a Christian church that offers special services to Outback Australians, periodically visit residents who live on remote stations. Ministering in this environment is challenging work and requires a special type of person. This is evident in the following job advertisement for a "minister on patrol," which appeared in the Uniting Church's *Frontier Services Bulletin* in November 2000:

"Position: Patrol Minister
Description: Must be prepared to travel around the far reaches of remote central Australia, through blinding dust storms, across swollen rivers that could wash you and the vehicle away, brave the blistering heat and severe thunderstorms to make contact with properties and communities not found on any existing map. Must have good sense of humour and stamina to deal with the frustration and inconvenience of trying to locate people and, when you do, the possible rejection. Must have compassion to share the hardships of the people, to counsel the grieving, to reconcile relationships, and be a very, very good listener. Must be able to perform marriages, baptisms and funerals. Accommodation is supplied but, most of your time, both waking and sleeping will be spent in a four-wheel drive. Good luck!"

picnic races held in the Outback. The Oak Park Races last for three days in July and have been held every year since 1904. Beginning in early July, station families prepare their horses to compete in the races, make trips to town to buy evening dresses for the dance, and assemble their camping gear.

Families come to the Oak Park Races from hundreds of miles away and set up large tents along the river. The main races are held in the mornings. During the afternoons, people visit each other or congregate in the main food tent, called the tucker tent, for a beer and conversation. On the evening of the second day of the races, an awards presentation dinner for the race winners and organizers is held. After the meal, there is a dance. The dance is a formal event where men wear coats, ties, and cowboy boots and women wear elegant evening gowns.

Picnic races like the Oak Park Races are an Outback tradition. People love them because they provide a welcome change from the hardships of station life and give neighbors a chance to get together and socialize. Mary Dixon of Bagstowe Station in Queensland says, "We [Outback families living on different homesteads] seldom see each other. The races offer the opportunity of a once a year reunion, of being able to forget the trials and tribulations of running a cattle property. It means being able to welcome old friends."[60]

Community Spirit

Not only at the races but year-round, deep and special friendships grow between station families in the Outback. They share the ups and downs when the seasons are uncertain and are united by common values and a shared purpose. Outback people take pride in their self-reliance, believe in their future, and are devoted to their life on the land.

At the root of it all is the family and the love of family members for each other. This makes people strong and gives their lives meaning and purpose. Terry Underwood describes her feelings about her community, her family, and their life in the Outback. She says:

> Our community is strong. This is the land where intimacy between the vibrant, innovative inhabitants defies the distances that separate us. There is a sense of trust and togetherness amongst Bushies [Outback people], whether experienced cattlemen or cattlewomen, first year jackeroos [trainee stockmen], retired weathered drovers [stockmen] or devoted governesses.... Our people are ... a breed apart—resourceful [and] resilient.... With faith, courage and determination we face the challenges of tomorrow. The strength of our community lies in the strength of our families. Our love for each other ... and the land we live in ... is ... powerful [and] ... eternal.[61]

CHAPTER

4 School by Air

Children in the Australian Outback often live hundreds of miles from regular schools and from each other. Providing quality education to those who live on remote sheep and cattle stations, in Aboriginal settlements, or in isolated mining communities is an enormous challenge. Determined that Outback children should not be disadvantaged by where and how their families live, Australian educators have developed some unique and innovative solutions to problems posed by distance and social isolation. Chris Tudor, who has taught Outback children for most of his career, puts it this way: "Here we are in the middle of nowhere. . . . If this place is to survive the kids must have the same opportunities as anywhere. . . . The whole thing is to break the shackles of isolation."[62]

Schools of the Air

Foremost among the innovative solutions developed by Australian educators are Outback Schools of the Air. These schools provide primary education based on correspondence courses. What makes them unique is that teachers and students communicate principally by two-way radio.

The first School of the Air was established in the 1950s in Alice Springs. This school was the first of its kind in the world. Adelaide Miethke from South Australia conceived of the idea in 1944 while visiting a remote Outback station as a member of the

council of the Royal Flying Doctor Service. Miethke was struck by how shy and isolated the children were and wrote in her memoirs:

> I looked around at the hard brown gibbers [boulders or stones] . . . at the scanty trees and the distant bush country. What a lonely spot. . . . Noticed a hen searching for food among the hard gibbers, and the thought came, "people live here." Then I caught sight of two sober little faces peeking round the corner of a building. . . . The picture of those two children, too shy to meet any stranger outside their own limited world, stayed with me.[63]

When she returned home, she suggested that the RFDS radio network be used to allow isolated students to communicate with trained teachers and with each other. Miethke's idea captured the imagination of South Australian educators. On June 8, 1951, the first School of the Air broadcast was made from the RFDS base in Alice Springs. Today there are sixteen Outback Schools of the Air. They teach children from four to thirteen years of age, or from preschool to seventh grade.

Student enrollment varies from forty students at Port Headland School of the Air in Western Australia, to about three hundred at the School of the Air in Katherine in the Northern Territory. However, all schools span vast distances of country and serve very isolated communities. With a broadcast area of eight hundred thousand square miles, the

Correspondence courses are often the only way Outback children receive their schooling.

School of the Air in Alice Springs, for example, boasts an enormous classroom. And when her children enrolled in the School of the Air in Katherine, one Outback mother said, "We were now part of a classroom four times the size of the United Kingdom. It was the biggest classroom in the world."[64]

Correspondence Materials

Correspondence materials written by government education departments form the basis of the curriculum for the schools.

However, School of the Air teachers adapt these materials to suit the needs of each student. Because class sizes are small, usually between seven and twelve students, teachers give students highly personalized attention, come to know them very well, and learn their strengths and weaknesses. Geoff O'Mallee, a public relations consultant for the Alice Springs School of the Air, says: "Our teachers tailor Northern Territories [Education Department] materials to student needs. It is a very personal style of education. . . . Our teachers get to know every child as an individual and can treat them as such."[65]

Schools of the Air are complex operations. Materials tailor-made for each student are packaged and sent out sometimes six months in advance to take into account poor weather conditions in the Outback. Computers, radios, and videocassette players are distributed to some families as well. And at the beginning of the year, librarians mail each student about sixteen books for reference and general reading; a computer tracking system keeps records of the large number of items out on loan. The mail room at the School of the Air in Katherine, for example, distributes more than seventy thousand items annually and looks like a small post office.

Every day Australia's Outback postal service takes mailbags containing correspondence lessons for children enrolled in the School of the Air to remote locations all over the Outback. Mailbags contain new work, answers for tutors, and video- and audiocassettes to be used as learning aids. Illustrations—designed, printed, and mailed weeks ahead of the relevant radio lesson—are used like a blackboard in conventional schools.

Students return a completed set of work every two weeks. Their work is graded by teachers and returned with a report, award certificates, and supplementary reading material. The reports and the rewards help motivate students who are so far away from their teachers. One Outback mother said, "The teacher wrote comments around scratch and smell stickers on various pages. Although

Traveling Play Groups

Because children on Outback stations live so far away from each other, they rarely have the chance to play together. Frontier Services, an organization run by the Uniting Church, wants to change this for preschool children in Outback Queensland with the Remote Area Families' Service (RAFS). As representatives of this organization, early childhood development specialists visit families living in isolated areas. They assess the progress of young children and discuss early childhood development concerns with parents. They also conduct playgroups to give children the opportunity to socialize with other children who are not their brothers and sisters.

Generally RAFS teams comprise two teachers. In an average week, the teachers might drive a thousand miles, conduct two playgroups of five to fifteen children, make several home visits to monitor child development, and attend a get-together of up to one hundred children organized by the School of the Air. Teachers drive a four-wheel-drive vehicle packed with toys, play equipment, and a portable adventure playground with mini-slippery slide. On weekends teachers often take their mobile classroom to rodeos and races, wherever Outback people congregate socially.

Work hours are long, and frequently RAFS teams find themselves lost, bogged in mud, stranded by overflowing creeks, hot, dusty, and frustrated trying to locate a family at a remote Outback station. However, the rewards of their work are many. The teams are highly appreciated by Outback parents who welcome being able to discuss their children's development. But the greatest reward of all comes from the excitement and delight of the children at the sight of the muddy vehicle packed with toys, and the satisfaction of seeing the very shyest Outback child run to join other children in play.

rather sickly sweet, the raspberry, cherry and banana odours proved great incentives."[66]

Home Classrooms

With their lessons in hand, children are ready to participate in their daily classes. A special area is set aside in the homestead or settlement to be used as the classroom. This can be a separate building, a separate room, or an area of an existing room. Regardless of location, the main object is to delineate the space from the rest of the homestead and community so that when children step into that area, they feel as though they are at school.

Schoolrooms are equipped with a two-way radio, desks, bookshelves, and sometimes a computer and audio- and videocassette players. Most parents try to make the classroom look and feel like an ordinary school classroom. One Outback mother recalls: "Our school room . . . was vibrant. Its walls were adorned with every imaginable art and craft work and gymkhana [rodeo] ribbons accumulated over the years when ponies Denim, Boxing Gloves, Tit and Whiskey carried their riders around barrels and pegs. Show awards and merit cards covered every spare space."[67]

Children with Disabilities

Educating children with learning difficulties or disabilities poses great hardships for families living in remote parts of the Outback. In her book *In the Middle of Nowhere*, Terry Underwood, an Outback mother from a remote cattle station in the Northern Territory, says parents with children who have special problems are often forced to leave the Outback and move to towns where they can get support for their children's needs:

"When things went wrong in the bush [Outback], help was a long way away. Young children with a physical impairment or learning disability created enormous pressures on bush families. Talented and gifted children were not catered for either. Distance and limited resources hijacked every agenda. We knew of broken families as a result or alternatively a family in need of full-time guidance exchanging station life for a town existence."

Radio Lessons

The school day usually begins with radio lessons. These are thirty minutes long and start with roll call. After roll call, teachers ask whether students have anything to report. They encourage students to share news about their lives. Terry Underwood transcribed one conversation between her nine-year-old son, Michael, and his teacher, Mr. Nepia. The teacher began:

"Good morning all grade four children. This is Mr. Nepia calling. Today I want you to tell me about your favorite pet. What is its name and what is its favorite trick? Firstly we'll go out west, almost as far as the West Australian border, to Riveren and to Michael Underwood. Go ahead Michael."

"Good morning Mr. Nepia. We have lots of pets but our blue heeler [cattle dog] Cuddles is the cleverest because she can ride a horse by herself. Over."

"Well there's no doubt about the Underwoods. Next they'll be telling us that Cuddles runs the stock camp."[68]

A child sits at his desk with his course material. His instruction takes place by way of radio.

After roll call, teachers conduct a question and answer session. These sessions are designed to develop ideas and concepts taught in the correspondence work. For example, radio lessons on Mondays for fifth grade (ten-year-olds) develop vocabulary and oral reading skills; on Tuesday, math; on Wednesday, social studies; and on Thursday, language and verbal expression. Friday is special library lesson day. The radio is also used for elective courses such as cooking, first aid, drug awareness programs, stamp collecting, art, and music. Australian author Thomas Keneally transcribed a typical question and answer session designed to reinforce a history lesson:

Teacher: Now what is the Ghan?

A number of lights come up on the teacher's console as children are pressing their buttons. The teacher switches to one of these lights.

Teacher: Yes, Peter.
Peter: A train, over.

Teacher: That's right. Now true or false. Alice Springs was founded because the Ghan came off the tracks and people had nowhere to live. (Again a glitter of lights.)

Teacher: Yes, Warren.
Warren: True, miss, over.
Teacher: Do you agree with that? Susan?
Susan: I think it's false, over.
Teacher: That's right.[69]

Communication Technology

Radio lessons, however, are often hampered by poor radio reception, which can be caused by bad weather or faulty generators. Sometimes, when children on distant stations are experiencing difficulties, they cannot hear some of

A student at a School of the Air in Queensland, speaks into a hand-held two-way radio.

their classmates. In the following example, Tim (grade seven) from Singleton Station in the Northern Territory was participating in a radio play and could not hear one of the other students who was also in the play. Geoff O'Mallee describes the situation:

> The students were performing a radio play using HF short wave radio. Unfortunately for Tim, he was unable to hear one of the other characters who seemed almost invariably to have the speaking part just before him. Tim, unable to hear the lines preceding his, was forced to read those lines to himself and to judge when his turn to speak came. He did very well, only being prompted twice by the teacher who was unaware of the difficulty Tim was having.[70]

Because of problems like these, Schools of the Air continually look to adapt new technology to improve the delivery of distance education. Since the late 1990s computers have been provided to families with children in fourth grade (nine-year-olds) or higher. New phone links set up in the early 1990s allow teachers to directly contact homes. Schools also run their own Internet service providers, and faxes are used to exchange information and samples of students' work.

But while phones, faxes, and computers are useful tools, educators still believe the radio is most successful at encouraging interaction between the teacher and students and students and their classmates. Administrators at Alice Springs School of the Air conclude that even with all the new technology and the problems with radio reception, "the ability to share news, experiences, the good times, sad times, happy events and just say 'G'day' is still best served by our old friend 'the radio.'"[71]

Home Tutors

Once the radio lesson is over, home tutors, who are usually parents, take over. Because they live in such isolated communities, Outback parents are intimately involved with their children's education.

Schools of the Air provide home lesson timetables to guide tutors by showing the amount of time to be spent on each activity each day. For example, the lesson timetable for a typical day for fifth-grade students includes a 30-minute radio session and 10 minutes of reading, 50 minutes of math, 150 minutes of English, 60 minutes of science, and 15 minutes of physical education. Such strict guidelines are the norm for Outback schools. Students are expected to work twenty-five hours a week, or five hours a day.

In most cases, the job of home tutor falls to mothers, but about 30 percent of families employ a governess to supervise the children's schoolwork. Governesses are usually young women who have just finished school or college and are trying to decide what to do with their lives. However, in many cases governesses

Challenges for Home Tutors

The job of home tutor is difficult for many parents, and some find the volume of work and new technology overwhelming. Sometimes Outback parents voice their concerns in letters to *Pedals*, the magazine of the Isolated Parents and Children's Association. In the following letter, which appeared in the March 2001 edition, Raelene Hall from Western Australia gives her views on the challenges of being a home tutor:

"The year 2001 will see me begin my eleventh year as Home Tutor. I will be starting again with a Year 1 child having seen two boys off to Boarding school. With that many year's experience, one would think that I would be feeling very confident about the prospect of teaching my daughter for the next seven years. The truth is I am feeling more daunted than ever.

In the years I have been teaching, I have seen the curriculum change several times, and in my opinion not always for the better. The work I have received for my Year 1 is, frankly, to me quite frightening. I hate to think how a new home tutor might be feeling. The sheer volume of material has to be seen to be believed. Books inches thick, guides for this and notes for that, videos, tapes, charts just to list a few. I keep pulling it out and putting it away because I really don't know where to start. . . .

Not only is there a new curriculum and format to deal with but technology is bringing changes for distance education as well. We need to ensure our children are not being left behind in the world of technology so we are trying to teach them how to use computers, when some of us only have a basic knowledge ourselves. . . . We must try to keep up with the times and ensure our children have access to the best education, but it is necessary to remember that the majority of Home Tutors out there . . . are not trained teachers and need all the help they can get."

find life in the Outback to be too hard and do not stay long.

Drawbacks of Home Tutoring

Whether run by parents or governesses, home tutoring has some disadvantages. One of the biggest challenges is maintaining discipline in the classroom. Lyn Conway from King's Creek Station in Central Australia recalls her experience:

> The thing I found very hard was keeping the kids focused. . . . It's difficult to try and motivate because you're so busy with everything else. For the first few years I was the teacher, and it was really tough be-

cause I had a baby [Sally]. . . . I didn't realize how easy [the eldest child] Megan was to teach, because Simon was off with the fairies. Megan was pretty self-motivated. Simon wasn't. Even in his radio lesson, he'd be under the desk and on top of the desk. He wasn't interested, and if I had to go out for any reason, out of that classroom, they were gone. They'd be gone for the day and I'd think, oh, this is terrible.[72]

Discipline is not the only problem Outback parents have schooling their children. Many parents also feel ill-equipped to supervise some of the lessons. Conway recalls trying to teach science to her youngest daughter, Sally: "Some of the subjects were quite involved. In science we had to do experiments,

Aboriginal children in the Northern Territory are being taught to read with the aid of their home tutor.

and none of our experiments ever worked. . . . The kids used to laugh and laugh. . . . I'm not very good at maths. . . . so Sally hates science and maths . . . Poor Sal, she'd struggle along."[73]

Problems faced by home tutors are compounded in Aboriginal communities. Often Aboriginal parents lack a basic education themselves, and for many Aboriginal people, English is their second, third, or even fourth language. Because correspondence materials are in English, there is little chance Aboriginal parents can supervise the lessons. This problem was highlighted in a national inquiry into distance education conducted in 2000. The inquiry concluded that Aboriginal people have not participated in a meaningful way in School of the Air programs mainly because "parents perceive their lack of literacy and numeracy skills as barriers to their children's participation in such programs."[74]

Another concern for both Aboriginal and nonindigenous children is that they have few opportunities to interact socially with people outside their own family or with children their own age. Many Outback children have no experience cooperating in a group. Liz Tier, a boarding school public relations officer, says children from remote areas can find "socializing a problem. Many of the children have never played a team sport. They are used to being with adults and find it hard to interact with their peers."[75]

Innovative Responses

These concerns do not go unnoticed by the Schools of the Air. In an effort to solve the problems, special programs have been developed to train home tutors, to address problems of Aboriginal children, and to provide opportunities for social interaction.

Schools of the Air play a vital role in the professional development of home tutors.

Since the success of homeschooling relies so heavily on the tutors, schools throughout the Outback organize an annual home tutors' conference at the beginning of each year to explain course objectives and lessons and demonstrate how to use materials. This conference guides parents in how to deal with discipline difficulties and any other problems they may have. One Outback mother recounts her experience at the conference at the School of the Air in Katherine in the Northern Territory:

> In Katherine, [at] the annual supervisors' conference for teacher-parents [home tutors] . . . we parents and supervisors attended lectures and discussions led by teachers and experts on every conceivable topic. Panels were formed and ideas and methods exchanged to make life in the home classroom effective and harmonious.[76]

Teacher Patrols

Further assistance is given to home tutors during teacher patrols. At least once a year, teachers visit every student and stay overnight at the child's station or community. Arriving around lunchtime, teachers carry out a school program for the rest of the day and the next morning. They assess working conditions, test the progress of their students, and listen to a radio lesson to judge the child's responses and the radio reception.

Patrols serve both professional and social needs. During the visits, teachers learn something personal about each child. They might meet a favorite pet or visit a special place around the homestead. In the process, a warm and close relationship develops. After dinner, teachers sit with parents and tutors, answer questions, and offer reassurance

Many Aborigines believe their people need an education system that both supports Aboriginal culture and imparts skills so their children can get jobs in mainstream society. Schools of the Air and traditional Australian schooling methods, however, have had limited success in educating Aboriginal children. Thus Aboriginal educators now rely on new approaches, including employing traditional teaching techniques (like storytelling) in a modern setting, using Aboriginal languages in schools, and sensitizing nonindigenous teachers to the culture. For example, Aboriginal students are generally very shy and do not like to stand out even for excellent work. Teachers thus learn to give praise discreetly, so as not to embarrass students and inhibit their performance at school.

Incorporating all of these ideas, Aborigines have set up new schools such as the Koori Open Door Education School in Victoria and Yipirinya Secondary College in Alice Springs. These schools recognize the link between culture and obtaining skills for jobs, and bring together the best in Aboriginal and non-Aboriginal teaching and learning methods. Aboriginal educators believe an education system that builds on respect for their traditions and heritage has the best chance of success.

School-age Aboriginal boys pose for the camera.

about the child's progress. These visits give the teachers a special appreciation of each student's predicament. An Alice Springs School of the Air publication notes: "The realization by teachers that some lessons must be [learned] in conditions of extreme discomfort—temperatures of [110 degrees] or more, constant dust, and distraction from siblings—leads to greater empathy and understanding of learning conditions from place to place."[77]

For Aboriginal students, a high level of additional support is necessary. Teachers skilled in teaching English as a second language go on patrol to Aboriginal settlements three times a year, once every term. These specialist teachers run intensive training programs for home tutors and work closely with all members of the community. They strive to improve the literacy and mathematical skills of the group. In this way, parents are more likely to encourage their children to learn.

Today many Aboriginal parents see the value of their children both learning their traditional laws and having a modern education. One Aboriginal grandmother put it this way:

> Long time ago my grandmother teaching [her] own way, culture way and that's way I'm teaching my grandchild. Make it strong; look after traditional culture, really strong way. . . . [Today] children [also should] go to school and learning whitefella way. Whitefella school important because the little one can't listen English properly, they need learning English for two way, for learning work, for money line, when they grow up so they can get a job. There's two way, traditional way and money line.[78]

Get-Togethers

To address problems incurred by social isolation and to give children a chance to interact with their peers, Schools of the Air organize regular get-togethers. For example, in February, the beginning of the Australian school year, students come to the School of the Air in Alice Springs to meet their teacher and classmates. In the middle of the year, get-togethers feature group sports and class excursions, and Christmas provides an opportunity for plays and festivities. Says Geoff O'Mallee, "For many children, this is their first experience of playing with other children

. . . and offers the chance to put faces to voices they've heard so often on the radio."[79]

Teachers also organize weeklong minischools usually once a year somewhere central to where most of their students live. Minischools are conducted like traditional day schools and are designed to give students a more normal school experience. During minischool, teachers also have the opportunity to tutor students in subjects like computer studies, music, drama, and physical education, which cannot be effectively taught over the air.

In the later grades, children go on excursions to different parts of Australia. For example, sixth- and seventh-grade students of the School of the Air in Alice Springs went on a weeklong trip to Cairns in Queensland in September 2001. These excursions expose children to the way other Australians live and help them feel part of the larger community.

High School Alternatives

Get-togethers and excursions are designed to prepare students for entry into a regular classroom situation in secondary school. The secondary school system is very different from the Schools of the Air. Students have two options. A small number of children choose to remain at home and complete their high school through correspondence courses run by the Northern Territory Open Education Center in Darwin. Some families feel this is the best option for station life. Three generations of the Emmot family of Noonbah, a cattle station in Queensland, have been educated at home entirely through correspondence courses. "For this type of life, it's a better education," contends Bruce Emmott. "If you want to be a doctor or lawyer, you have to go away. But for our life, you need a good education—I agree—but you need to adapt to life here."[80]

Most parents, however, send their children to secondary boarding schools. In Central Australia, for example, the majority of students go to boarding school in Alice Springs. And some parents choose to send their children to boarding schools in the major Australian cities of Adelaide, Sydney, Brisbane, or Melbourne.

Regardless of whether children go to an Outback or a big city boarding school, separation from their families causes great hardship and can be a very emotional time for parents and children. One Outback mother writes of her experience at the gates of her sons' boarding school:

> Everyone knew that to prolong the departure was to prolong the heartache. . . . It was important not to cry. Once I started crying I could not stop. For one who was supposed to lead by example in the bravery stakes, I was still learning to allow only inward tears to flow. . . . Our two young sons stood side by side, desperately trying to appear brave as goodbye time confronted them. . . . I thought I would choke emotionally. . . . These were the penalties for the freedom and independence of living in one of the most remote and beautiful parts of our vast continent.[81]

Difficult Adjustment

Once children arrive at boarding school, there is usually a period of adjustment to the people, routines, and confines of the classroom.

A teacher instructs pupils at a school in Alice Springs, Queensland. Aborigines are shy and often have difficulty adjusting to the social atmosphere of school.

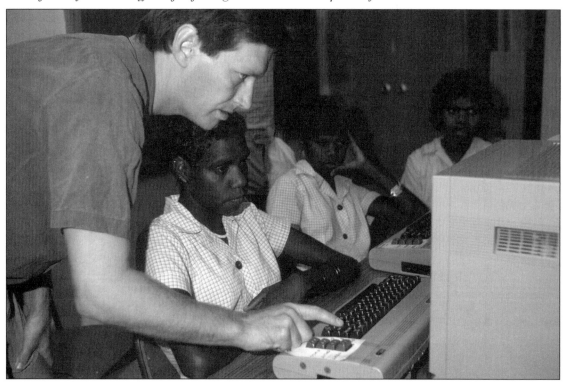

A Queensland farm boy lines up saddles on a fence. Outback children often feel like misfits in boarding schools.

Outback children face all sorts of difficulties. Many who have been around adults all their life find it hard relating to children their own age. In addition, most never learned how to play basketball or hopscotch or other childhood games. Furthermore, all the rules at school can be foreign to Outback children used to tremendous freedom. Jill Ker Conway, who grew up in Outback New South Wales, describes her first experience at boarding school: "I found the small world inside the school gates alien and intimidating. Having never had a playmate I did not know how to play. . . . I could not understand the point of physical exercise. . . . I knew how to do hard physical labor, but I was bored by phys. ed. classes and too clumsy to play the games."[82]

In big city boarding schools where there are few Outback students, Outback children often feel especially out of place. "We feel like misfits from the start. We find out our cowboy boots and jackets which we wore on the station aren't right for the city,"[83] one boy explained.

Quality Outback Education

Although the adjustment period can be difficult, Outback children usually settle into the boarding schools' routines and do very well. A maturity developed very early in life works to their advantage. Outback children are used to taking on responsibilities, completing tasks, and working with little supervision. During national standardized exams in third, fifth, and seventh grades, which test basic reading, writing, and arithmetic skills, most Outback students consistently perform above the national average. And at the high school level they generally do well. "Our kids leave here and go to universities all over Australia,"[84] says Chris Tudor, headmaster of the Outback College in Alice Springs.

Thanks to boarding schools and Schools of the Air, a quality education is within the reach of most Outback children. The determination of educators to diminish the disadvantages posed by physical distance and cultural isolation is showing good results.

Opal Fever

Opals are rare and beautiful gemstones that feature a kaleidoscope of colors. Australia's Outback is home to more than 90 percent of the world's opals. People come from all over the globe hoping to strike opal and make their fortune.

The work of opal mining is grueling and dangerous, conditions are harsh, and failure rates are high. Less than 5 percent of miners ever strike it rich. However, fascination with the gemstone is at the root of "opal fever," which compels miners to risk life and limb and suffer many hardships in pursuit of the treasured gems. According to writer Patrick O'Brien, when opal fever takes hold, "no waterless countryside is too barren or inhospitable, no opal level is too impenetrable and no risk of failure and consequent financial ruin is strong enough to sway them [miners] from their chosen path."[85]

Opal Towns

Australia's opal fields form a sweeping arc from the north of South Australia through northwest New South Wales into southwest Queensland. The major opal fields are adjacent to the opal mining towns of Coober Pedy, Mintabie, and Andamooka in South Australia, and Lightning Ridge and White Cliffs in New South Wales. A number of smaller opal fields are in southwest Queensland, including those near the towns of Opalton and Opalville.

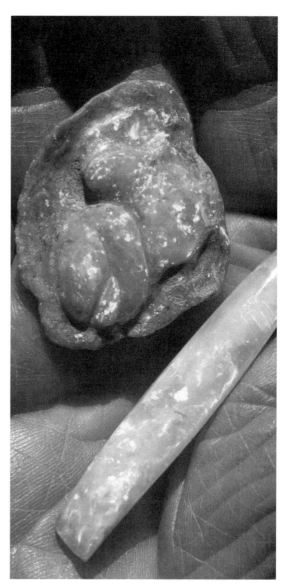

A miner holds raw opal gemstones found at Coober Pedy in South Australia.

Mining on Aboriginal Land

Not all Outback residents support opal mining. Because of the Aborigines' special relationship with the land, their beliefs often come in conflict with the goals of miners and prospectors. In the course of mining for opals, gold, minerals, and precious gems, miners have destroyed many sacred Aboriginal sites. Because Aborigines believe the welfare of their people and all living things depends on their careful preservation of these sites, mining activities have caused them much grief.

After years of ignoring Aboriginal views, however, the Australian community as a whole is coming to show respect for the culture of the country's first inhabitants. In recognition of the rights of Aborigines to protect their sacred sites, miners now consult with tribal elders and seek permission to mine on their land. Miners also pay the Aborigines royalties when precious gems are found. Furthermore, to ensure that mining employees appreciate the Aboriginal viewpoint, companies are conducting cross-cultural training programs. In the East Kimberley Region of Western Australia, for example, the Argyle Diamond Mine runs a cooperative project with the Aboriginal owners of the area, the Gidja people. The Gidja people teach mine employees about the strong connections they have with the land and about their culture and traditions.

However, Aboriginal views are not always respected. There are still times when financial interests dominate the concerns of Australia's indigenous people. In 1998, for example, Aboriginal groups held widespread protests at a proposed uranium mine site at Jabiluka, in the Northern Territory. Despite these objections, government authorities agreed to the mining companies' claims, and plans for the mining of uranium are under way in the area.

The size and amenities of opal towns vary. Lightning Ridge, with an estimated six thousand people, has modern amenities such as schools, hospitals, motels, restaurants, supermarkets, communal swimming pools, and movie theaters. At the other end of the scale is Opalton, with a permanent population of twenty people; amenities in Opalton include only one general store, a gas station, and a solar-powered public phone booth.

Population statistics for mining towns are unreliable, because the towns have large transient populations. Miners come and go. Some miners run out of money before they strike opal and have to return to the cities to earn a living. Other residents leave during the hot summer months and return to mine in winter.

And numbers can swell overnight when anyone has a good opal find. Writer Robert Haill explains, "On the fields there can be . . . one lone miner. If that miner shouts 'OPAL,' within an hour that ground will be as busy as the Melbourne [capital of Victoria] Railway Station at peak hour. . . . A new site has been started."[86]

The Miners

Even though mining towns vary in size and amenities, they uniformly attract a multicultural community. As many as 75 percent of Outback opal miners are immigrants. This makes for a distinctive ethnic flair in opal towns. Voices of a dozen nationalities can be

A resident of Coober Pedy poses for a photo in his underground home.

heard singing in the streets at night in Coober Pedy, where more than fifty-three nationalities including Bosnians, Hungarians, Germans, Swiss, Chinese, and Japanese are represented. And advice on early mailing for Christmas appears in the post office in fifteen languages. Archie Kalokerinos, who mined for opal at Coober Pedy, said, "How the postmaster managed his business, I will never understand. Letters came addressed in Greek, Italian, German, English and practically any European language you care to name. And the spelling was often as puzzling as the language."[87]

These multicultural communities are tolerant of people's differences. Miners with varied backgrounds and eccentricities find they are welcomed into the community, accepted just as they are, and treated well. Frenchman Richard Malouk, who lives at Lightning Ridge with his German wife, says, "It is the people of Lightning Ridge who make it magic. Here if you are a good person you are treated equally. You are a local!"[88]

Miners' Homes

Like the people themselves, miners' homes are distinct and unusual. Living conditions of opal miners range from primitive tents to brick, sandstone, or underground structures. In general, an area's climate and resources determine the type of house that will be built there.

In some towns, Coober Pedy and White Cliffs particularly, temperatures are so extreme that homes are often built underground where the temperature stays a consistent 65 to 70 degrees. These underground homes are called dugouts. From the outside, dugouts look like small hills with entrance doors. From the inside, they look like regular houses, except they have rock walls and ceilings and no windows. Most dugouts are comfortably furnished and include modern conveniences. They generally have four or five rooms, but some dugouts look like mansions. These homes can be as large as twelve hundred square feet and may even include swimming pools.

Not all opal towns have ground suitable to support dugouts, though, so miners come up with other often unconventional building materials. Lightning Ridge, for instance, is home to some of the most unusual structures in the world. One journalist from *Australian Geographic* said: "There are houses made of beer bottles, a drive-in mine, full-scale castles, an enormous homemade observatory and a Museum housing the donated pickled body parts of accident prone miners. Lightning Ridge boasts a quality of eccentricity that astonished me."[89] Many miners, however, choose not to build permanent homes. Instead, they live on the opal fields next to the towns. They live in tents, tin sheds, trailers, or hastily erected shelters made with whatever material is lying around. Living conditions on the fields are primitive, and there is no electricity or running water. Miner Barbara McCondra recalls her living conditions on the opal fields of Coocoran, near Lightning Ridge: "I lived under a tree for a couple of years. My home was a bent piece of tin and a mining ladder, and I slept in my car. . . . My pantry was the tree, for all my pots and pans hung on that tree."[90]

Miners' Kindness

Mining conditions in the Outback are harsh, but miners say this is counterbalanced by the special kindness and concern miners have for each other. In *Opals of the Never Never*, Robert Haill tells the story of an elderly opal miner at Coober Pedy in South Australia:

"There was this old Hungarian called Pink Eyes who had been on the field for years, noodling [looking for opal chips] through the dumps [rubble]. Now and then the miners felt sorry for him and dropped, unnoticed, a small opal into his dilly-bag [rucksack]. One day [in the rubble] he found a 16 ounce piece of seam opal in an open cut and sold it for $5000. Then he quietly went around the huts of the miners who had been kind to him, leaving envelopes of money to repay their help, and left the fields, never to be seen again."

Divining for Opal

The reason most miners do not set up elaborate living arrangements is that their main focus is on mining for opal. Once their camp is established, the miners' first task is to decide where to dig. Often this is a difficult decision, because there is no sure way of knowing where opal can be found. Says one veteran miner, "There is one question that can never be accurately answered. Where is the best place to find opal? Every miner has scratched his head when he has had to choose a new site."[91]

Opals are generally found between one and one hundred feet belowground, and sometimes miners recognize surface features that may indicate there is opal beneath them. For example, flat-capped sandstone hills can be a sign that there are opals in the area. The presence of pink or reddish bands of sandstone wedged between the dirt suggests there might be vertical faults underground that may contain opal. Haill says, "The ground tells a story. It slides and runs in levels and a good miner can read the ground. The ability to recognize 'probable' ground comes with experience."[92]

Once miners have established that they are on opal-bearing country, they have to decide where to dig. "Divining" is one of the most common methods miners use to decide where to drill their shaft. To divine for opals, miners hold wire rods parallel to each other at waist height and walk across the ground. The rods detect electromagnetic currents in faults below the surface. These currents sometimes cause the rods to cross. Most miners who use divining rods try to locate these faults because opal is often found along fault lines. However not all faults contain opal, and divining rods do not uncover precious opal most or even much of the time. So over the years miners usually work multiple claims.

Staking a Claim

Once an area has been selected, miners must purchase a permit to dig from the government. These permits, called precious stones prospecting permits, cost about twenty-two dollars and last for twelve months. Miners must also pay a claim fee, which costs nine dollars for an area 150 by 150 feet, or eighteen dollars for an area 150 by 300 feet in most mining areas, though in Queensland, the size of the claim is not restricted. Buying a permit and paying the claim fee means that a miner has a right to that claim, and no one else can dig there. Miners identify their claims with numbered tags placed on pegs at each of the four corners.

Pegging a claim can mean a lot to miners. Some believe it puts them well on their way to making their fortunes. Stephen Aracic recalls: "John, a mate of mine, came to Lightning Ridge in late March 1992. There was just

A man divines for underground minerals at the site of an opal mine in Coober Pedy.

himself and his cat. . . . He decided to peg a claim when he selected a piece of ground he liked and I surveyed it for him. John was so excited about his acquisition. He could live on his piece of land, mine for opal and become a millionaire, or so he thought."[93]

Mining Methods

With their claims pegged and registered, miners begin to dig. They choose one of two methods of mining for opals. The method of choice depends on the terrain and on a miner's financial resources.

The open-cut method is used on opal fields where opal is found in isolated pockets close to the surface. In this method, several people work together on one claim. Giant tungsten rippers or metal prongs on the back of huge bulldozers slice through the ground. The rippers rip to a depth of about a foot. Miners called checkers walk behind the dozer and watch the ground for any opal traces. If they see opal, the checkers then signal the driver, who stops the machine so the opal can be dug out by hand. The bulldozer then moves over a foot or two, and the next rip begins. This process continues over the entire digging area.

After the bulldozer has completed the ripping for one level, the broken-up sandstone from the ripping is then pushed aside by the blade of the bulldozer or taken out by a machine called a scraper. Checkers constantly follow the dozer looking for traces of opal. When the floor for the first cut has been cleaned, the whole ripping process is repeated until the bulldozer finishes the cut to an agreed depth. This might be anywhere up to one hundred feet below the ground's surface and depends on the miner's judgment on the likelihood of finding opals.

Open-cut mining is effective but costly. Because an open-cut miner cannot work alone, one or more checkers must be employed. A truck driver also has to be hired to cart hundreds of drums of fuel and water from town for use at the work site. Large bulldozers and tunneling machines use great quantities of diesel fuel, and it can take a long time to complete a cut. Cuts on the Mintabie field, for example, are made to a depth of about eighty feet. This process can take between three and six months to complete. And as a rule, opal deposits are patchy and located by trial and error. Robert Haill says, "Sometimes it can cost $10,000 to find $10 of opal by open cut mining."[94]

Underground Mining

Because the costs involved in open-cut mining are so high, most miners work underground. Miners dig shafts with automatic drills that can make holes about three feet in diameter and ninety feet deep in three hours. Once underground, miners often use jackhammers to remove the bulk of the sandstone they encounter. Power winches, self-tipping hoists, and sometimes truck-mounted blowers, which operate like giant vacuum cleaners, remove the dirt.

Although some miners just use jackhammers, in most cases they also use explosives to make their shafts. These explosives produce dangerous fumes, which can be deadly to humans. Thus, miners have to let the fumes clear before they begin to mine. Some miners hasten the process by using ventilation machines to clear the fumes quickly.

Miners usually work in pairs. One works below digging the ground, filling the buckets, and detonating the explosives. The other works above, manning the hoist to bring up

A miner inspects a mound of rock and dirt taken by hoist from the mine below.

the dirt and send down the tools and explosives. Workdays are long and physically demanding. Miner Peter Blythe describes his daily routine:

> My average day . . . I was filling up about 350 twelve gallon drums full of dirt and then wheel-barrowing them fifty feet and filling them up again and doing that every day all day. . . . I go to work [149 pounds] and come home [6.5 pounds] lighter. . . . Underground you're in your jocks [underpants] and you just sweat and it runs off you. . . . You have to be a masochist, because it's a lot of pain and you've got skinned knuckles all day and things like that.[95]

Dangers on the Field

The hard labor is made more difficult by the harsh conditions of the mine fields. Miners constantly grapple with flies and dust. When the wind picks up, dirt blows into every pore of their bodies, and flies come out to absorb any moisture from their perspiration. Furthermore, the work itself is very dangerous.

One of the most obvious hazards comes with the constant use of explosives. Miners sometimes use explosives four or five times a day to excavate underground tunnels. Up to sixteen explosive charges are placed in drill holes at an average depth of three to four feet. These are lit one at a time and are counted above ground as they explode. Any shot that does not go off can leave a live detonator that could explode if disturbed. Thus, miners carefully remove any unexploded shot. Fuses are also lit very slowly so that each explosion can be heard and counted. One miner's wife explained:

> You don't just light one, then another really quickly and come up, you have to light one fuse [and wait several seconds before lighting the next fuse]. Then when the sixteen are lit, there is barely time to make it up the [ninety-foot] ladder to the top with the shaft filling up with smoke. I'm always glad to see him [my husband] come up.[96]

Explosives are not the only danger, though. When miners find opal, they often dig out a large area underground, which is called a ballroom. The ballroom is usually the size of an average living room, about fifteen feet by fifteen feet. Its ceiling is often only a few inches higher than the miner is tall and is supported by wooden beams or dirt pillars. Miners who do not adequately support the ballroom's ceiling are vulnerable to cave-ins. One miner says:

> I noticed this bloke [man] sitting close by on a mullock [rock] heap. And he was ghastly white. His hair was actually standing up. I had thought at the time gee this bloke looks crook [sickly]. What had taken place out there was this bloke . . . had asked permission to go down the other miner's claim beside us. He had started gouging [digging] underground

A sign warns of explosives and open shafts around a mining area.

when he heard noises coming from our end. The props [wooden beams supporting the shaft] had started popping [collapsing], and when they do the noise is indescribable as it echoes through the tunnels. There had been two men down there. They high tailed it quick smart up that ladder, just as the roof caved in around them. They had almost been buried alive.[97]

Most miners also have close calls with faulty equipment. Miners' personal safety depends on their equipment working well, and when it fails miners can face life-threatening situations. Lew Wilson of Lightning Ridge describes one near-fatal accident involving his brother John:

The bucket, filled with dirt . . . is really heavy. The hoists are designed to keep going up or down, regardless. One day my brother John [working underground] reached over to pull the hoist into gear. Suddenly the rope caught on his arm, enough to lift him off the ground. He started to get pulled up the shaft by his arm, and we couldn't free him. Another friend, Barry, grabbed the bucket, and with both John and Barry's weight on the

An opal miner prepares to place explosives in an underground shaft.

bucket, they still couldn't hold it down. Up and up it went with John now three feet off the ground, and being drawn further and further up the shaft [which was getting narrower and narrower]. I rushed around and grabbed the lever and pulled it out of gear. John fortunately survived that ordeal, however had we not been able to free him, he would have been crushed to death [by the walls of the shaft].[98]

Even though the work poses many dangers and hardships, miners develop an attachment to their work environment. The explosions and large machines whirring and clanking on the opal fields create a special atmosphere. Of the fields at Lightning Ridge, Robert Haill says:

The place has something about it. The sounds of bedlam on the fields with the eardrum-splitting cacophony of grinding, whirring, belching humming noises associated with opal mining. The incessant unmelodious wail of horns and sirens signaling winches to be started, hoist drums stacked with explosives to be lowered. Hard-hatted miners pop out of holes like rabbits to the rumble of chain explosions as their explosives blast out drives, pulverising everything in the way, ripping boulders down, widening shafts. The deafening roar of nitro-pill thunders like tank fire. Then the hard hats disappear back down the shafts.[99]

Harsh Living Conditions

Miners' hardships are not confined to the work of mining. Living conditions are also difficult. Heat, flies, whirling dust storms, and venomous snakes and spiders are just some of the hazards. When added to the lack of amenities on the fields, life is very challenging. Pat Gregory says of the Opalton fields, "There's no drinking water, no fresh food, no electricity and no authority. . . . This is tough back-breaking country where everything has to be done manually. . . . Out here on the opal fields the living conditions are harsh."[100]

Extreme heat is a primary concern. Temperatures on opal fields can be more than 100 degrees for thirty days at a time. Summer temperatures in Coober Pedy have been known to reach 130 degrees, and conversations among the locals often revolve around the heat; people discuss whether the next day will be baking hot, blistering hot, scorching hot, or just plain hot.

Blinding dust storms, drought, and poisonous creatures are also problematic. In particular, massive gusts of swirling red dust known as a willy-willy cause havoc for residents. And in Opalton, residents say that *rain* is a four-letter word used about twice a year. Haill says:

There is much to discourage the opal miner. Look out at the spinning dust on the horizon: a willy-willy. The skies darken as a blinding dust storm sweeps across the desert. The lazy nagging buzz of the bush flies crawling into ear and mouth searching for moisture. The almost transparent [six-inch] scorpions climb into boots and sleeping bags and drop down shafts seemingly to wait for a miner to come down. The venomous snakes, the bindi-eye [prickly] thorn creeper that tangles around feet and legs, and the millions and millions of gibbers [stones] rolling underfoot.[101]

Raising Children

The most vulnerable residents are often the children who accompany their parents to the

Miners drill a hole into a wall of an opal mine in Coober Pedy.

opal fields. Water is scarce, and the water that is available is high in nitrates, which poses a health hazard for children under three. In addition, hundreds of abandoned open shafts on the mine fields pose a major hazard. Many children have disappeared and been found at the bottom of a shaft. One miner's wife remembers:

Fiona nearly lost her life at the age of two years. She accidentally fell into a shaft [nine feet] deep and half full of wa-

ter. . . . Not waiting to remove my shoes, I scrambled down the rough wall and slid into the water to pick her up. Sheer determination to get her out alive gave me added strength. With one mighty heave I propped my back against the wall, my feet against the other side. I tilted her body across my knees to clear her air passage of water. Fortunately she began to cough and splutter almost immediately because of the short time in the water.[102]

Even with all these hazards, miners' families, children included, love their way of life. Children and their parents value their freedom living in the Outback away from the hustle and bustle of the cities. Peter Blythe's wife, Ann, says, "After all, freedom is ours away from the stress and strains of city life. We love the way of life, the atmosphere and the freedom from pressures and world problems.

How can a miner ever return to that sort of life [city life] after experiencing opal mining?"[103]

Ratters

Natural dangers are not the only hazards for miners and their families. The remote location of many mining towns and camps and the lure

Women opal miners stand in front of a hoist dumping new dirt pulled from the ground.

of great riches attract thieves and undesirable characters. Gemologist Fred Ward says:

> The Ridge [Lightning Ridge] is a hideaway for loners, a place for getting lost. In fact I suspect the vast majority of its miners first came to the Ridge to escape—something or someone—and stayed to dig opal. Folks go by their first names—or aliases—keep no records, and guard information. Opal is an all-cash business, an on-the-spot done-deal, settled with a pile of A[Australian] $50 or $100 [notes] and no paperwork.[104]

People in mining towns and camps keep details of their lives private; many do not even acknowledge their own existence on public records. For example, even though only sixteen hundred people were on the electoral roll in 1998 at Lightning Ridge, bread sales and post office pickups suggested that up to eight thousand people lived there.

As a result, the world of opal miners is a secretive one that is unregulated by government or tax authorities. In this environment, the lure of instant wealth sometimes draws criminals who prey on honest miners. Opal thieves are called ratters because they are known to fight like rats in a trap if they get caught in the underground mines. Ratters often go into miners' claims at night to steal their opals, and while some work alone, others are part of well-organized groups.

Ratters have been known to go to great lengths to steal precious opal. One veteran miner recalls:

> Two miners were working their opal productive claim at the Four Mile [at Lightning Ridge]. . . . It was during the peak of opal mining when they were getting millions of dollars worth of opal. . . . They were using a blower and a 20-tonne [ton] truck. The miners would load a truck full of opal dirt daily, then drive it to the puddling dam [water catchment area] for processing. One day the worst possible thing happened to them. They came out of the shaft to drive the truck away. Lo and behold there was no truck there. Thieves had stolen the full load![105]

Mini-Miner

Some children develop a taste for the mining life from an early age. Eleven-year-old Troy Markham, from the opal mining town of Lightning Ridge in northern New South Wales, went down a shaft for the first time when he was eight years old. He tells his story in Rusty Bowen's *Miners' Tales from the Black Opal City*:

"The first time I went down a mine shaft, dad put a safety helmet on me, and gave me strict safety rules to go by. He stayed right underneath me on the ladders just in case I slipped. I got down to the bottom of the shaft and I looked around me. It was fantastic! This was like another world. I was only little, so I was a bit scared, and excited at the same time I guess.

Using a jack hammer for the first time, I shook more than it did. I wasn't big enough to use it correctly, so it didn't do much except shake the life out of me. I am interested in opal, and when I grow up I want to be a full time miner. I enjoy watching the professional opal cutters, and I've had a little practice myself. Everything about Lightning Ridge and opal, is really fascinating. I reckon without a doubt, that Lightning Ridge is the best place in the world."

Opal miners work hard but love to have fun, too. They enjoy playing sports like soccer and getting together to have barbecues. In an article called "Life in Mintabie: A Woman's View of the Opal Fields," published in the March 1984 edition of *Australian Gem and Treasure Hunter* magazine, Ann Blythe, an opal miner's wife, describes an Outback soccer match and feast held on a Saturday afternoon in the opal mining town of Mintabie in South Australia:

The [soccer field] is constructed by a bulldozer and then the men walk over it picking up the large boulders. . . . The fattest guy on the field gets to play goalkeeper. It is a fun match with not a lot of skill required. . . . The grand match is followed by . . . a pig on a spit plus a lamb, . . . expertly cooked by [miner and chef] Bruno and carved by Charlie the butcher. . . . Contrary to Bruno's approach (which is slow and precise), there is no time to stand back and examine the prey because of the swarms of flies that threaten to carry the pig away themselves. So with the help of six people all wafting paper plates in the hope of discouraging the flies, Charlie the butcher pulls the trotters [hoofs] and tail off and proceeds to carve into the tender flesh, at the same time encouraging the hungry crowd to feed themselves.

Frontier Justice

Some miners are so fed up with ratters that they have taken to protecting their claims with homemade booby traps. Some put snakes or attach poison-tipped nails to tunnel floors. Others set traps in shaft entrances or leave deep holes at the foot of ladders. Such measures often dissuade ratters from tampering with the miners' claims or in some cases can help miners catch ratters red-handed.

When ratters are caught, they are dealt with severely. Sometimes miners take the law into their own hands. For example, victimized miners at Lightning Ridge firebombed one ratter's house three times before he decided to leave town. If such tactics do not work, drive-by shootings are usually the next resort, which can be followed by more extreme measures. "If they [angry miners] catch you, they can put you down a hole and drop a stick of gelignite [explosive] on top of you," said one opal miner.

Opal miners persevere through harsh physical challenges because they believe their fortunes await them.

"No one would ever know. I am sure lots of people are buried on opal fields."[106]

Lure of the Life

Despite these dangers and hardships, miners continue to try their luck. They do so because some people succeed. About 5 percent become multimillionaires, and about 20 percent make a living at mining. All miners believe their fortunes are out there waiting for them. "I know there's one out there with my name on it," says Peter Blythe of his new claim. "I just haven't dug in the right hole yet."[107]

Blythe has the memory of a major opal find in Mintabie to keep him going. He and other miners report that there is nothing more thrilling than the discovery of precious opal. Blythe described this feeling as "opal ecstasy":

After the first [sight of opal] my legs went weak, the hair on my neck stood up and my hands began to shake. In less than an inch our thin trace had turned into beautiful green opal almost 5mm thick. All our aches and pains disappeared. Inside an hour we half filled a plastic bucket and the opal was still going. In fact it seemed to be getting thicker and the vein stretched the entire width of the drive ahead. By the end of the day we had completely filled two buckets and the opal was still going. . . . The next day the opal kept going (it begins to hurt when you grin continuously for three days).[108]

The thrill of the find attracts many people to the mining life. But even after years of no success, many continue to mine for opals. The allure of opal fever often proves irresistible. One miner from Lightning Ridge says, "I've been out here for 32 years now after only coming for a three-month visit. . . . I'm 62 and the rocks in my head [visions of opals] keep stopping me from retiring. . . . You always dream about what might be behind the next wall of dirt, the opal fever can drive you crazy."[109]

6 Outback Town Life

Outback towns are centers for social gatherings, focal points where station hands, miners, road and railway workers, and travelers come for fun, social life, and supplies. Writer Jocelyn Burt says, "[Outback towns like] Alice Springs [are] more than just [towns] in an ordinary sense. For [people living in remote parts of the Outback] they are . . . centres of civilisation in a wide, harsh land, . . . they are an oasis of friends and events."[110]

Hosting seasonal Outback events defines the rhythm of life in the towns. From May to September, the cooler winter months, Outback towns spring to life with unique and colorful festivities that reflect the humor and ingenuity of the people who live there, and define the character of the towns. Thousands of visitors are drawn every year to these festivities, and for many towns, tourism is the key to their survival.

Outback Towns

Dotted sparingly throughout the Outback, towns vary considerably in size, population, and facilities. From the largest town of Darwin in the Northern Territory with 82,400 people, to Innamincka in southwest Queensland, permanent population 12 people, Outback towns run the full gamut. Some of the larger towns are thriving modern metropolises, with large immigrant communities and sophisticated populations. Darwin, for example, is a bustling town with a young pop-ulation and a cosmopolitan atmosphere; it is home to more than forty-five ethnic groups. Alice Springs, with 25,000 people and the highest percentage of university graduates of all towns in Australia, is an upbeat sophisti-cated community on the go. The 3,700 residents of Broome in Western Australia include large numbers of Asians—Chinese, Japanese, Malaysian, and Philippinos—giving the town a particular character and flavor of its own. In contrast, Hall's Creek, the most isolated town in Western Australia, has 1,200 people, 70 percent of whom are Aboriginal, and Birdsville in Queensland has 120 people, many of whom are related.

Outback towns also offer a full range of facilities. Facilities in the large towns like Darwin and Alice Springs include those found in most modern cities. Alice Springs has more than twenty schools, a public hospital, a central business district with major shopping centers, extensive sporting facilities, theaters, libraries, and recreation centers. However, most Outback towns are much smaller and have limited facilities. These usually include a hotel and trailer park, a general store, a gas station, the local pub, and emergency services. Some Outback towns have little more than the local pub, which acts as a general store, gas station, and post office. One Outback jour-nalist describes the town of Koetong in Outback Victoria: "Koetong . . . is the Koetong pub. There's not much else—half a dozen houses perhaps, and not even a church. The last public building was the post office, which

Darwin is the largest town in Australia's Outback. It is home to more than forty-five ethnic groups.

closed in 1991. Even its public hall was relocated to [an adjoining town]."[111]

Similarities

Although Outback towns vary in size and facilities, they do have common characteristics. The most common is that they are remote, usually hundreds of miles from each other. For example, one has to travel almost a thousand miles from Alice Springs in central Australia to reach another town of any size. "We are a unique town because of our isolation. There is no one near us for [one thousand miles] in any direction,"[112] says Alice Springs director of tourism, Craig Catchlove.

Towns are also subject to the harsh climate and conditions characteristic of Outback Australia. Heat, dust storms, and extreme weather conditions like cyclones, floods, and hurricanes plague Outback towns and the people who live in them. Summers of 130-degree days are common. Marble Bar, a small town in Western Australia, is best known for being the hottest town in Australia, having recorded 136 days over 100 degrees in a row. And during the wet season, towns can be cut off from the outside world for weeks at a time. The mayor of Alice Springs, Fran Erlich, says, "It's hard to live in Outback towns—[with] the weather, the isolation." [113]

The weather and the seasons are such prominent factors in the Outback that they determine the rhythm of life in towns. When temperatures begin to dip below ninety degrees in March, there is a hum of excitement in towns all throughout the Outback as residents prepare for the influx of tourists and travelers.

During the tourist season, population levels of Outback towns fluctuate enormously. In Birdsville, for example, the usual 120 residents are joined by 5,000 visitors in September; Innamincka's population of 12 swells to more than 1,000 people as the town teams with stockmen, oil and road workers, and travelers for the picnic races in August; and Helenvale, a tiny Queensland town with a pub, 3 permanent residents, and little else, hosts 1,000 visitors a day from April to October.

Festivals and Races

For many towns, popular annual events attract these tourists and define the character of the town. "It is the various festivals during the year that perhaps best reflect the character of the town,"[114] says Jocelyn Burt.

The festivals are characterized by a unique brand of Outback humor and fun. The Alice Springs Camel Cup, for example, begins the tourist season in May. Camels from all over the Outback compete in Australia's biggest camel race. Despite months of preparation and the money at stake, the event is best known for its lighthearted Outback humor. Burt says:

A Birdsville resident refreshes with a beer under the hot Outback sun.

Camels are camels, and more often than not, when the starter's gun goes off, the animals simply refuse to get up. Then, if they decide to heed the frantic pleas of jockeys—and those of the equally frantic punters [bettors]—they are quite likely to bound off in a direction totally different from that of the set track. Although the race generally ends in chaos, nobody really minds. It's all good for a laugh.[115]

Another famous and humorous festival is the Henley-on-Todd Regatta, which is held in Alice Springs in late September. The regatta is a parody of the formal boat races held on the Thames River in England. The regatta in Alice Springs draws large crowds of people who come to watch bottomless boats raced down the normally dry Todd River bed. Boats are propelled by the crews' legs, which stick out as they run down the sandy course. Author Thomas Keneally describes the event:

Every August the town fathers of Alice Springs celebrate a regatta in the Todd River. With the sort of whimsical [oddball] humor which characterizes Australians in remote places, they call the event Henley-on-Todd and the [humor] consists of this: that the Todd only flows after rare heavy rain. The regatta is therefore held in the dry sand of the riverbed. The organizers yearly take out insurance against rain. To have water in the Todd would spoil the regatta, would send thousands of visitors away, would bring down commercial disaster.

The yachts which compete in Henley-on-Todd have sails but no keels. Squads of brawny central Australians step into them,

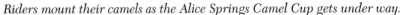

Riders mount their camels as the Alice Springs Camel Cup gets under way.

Members of one team, race across the sand with their canoe at the Henley-on-Todd Regatta.

lift them by means of bars running [across] the vessels, and take off with them, running in unison. The running has to be in time. If those who are carrying a yacht get out of step with each other, the craft will nose-dive into the sand, the runners in the stern will be projected backside over tip [head over heels] through the rigging, perhaps headfirst through the mainsail. . . . The crews project them by digging deep into the sand with paddles. It is all done in great heat with preposterous energy.[116]

The regatta and camel races are just two of hundreds of unusual festivals and races held throughout the Outback. Australians love to gamble, and even small Outback towns host thousands of visitors for races of all kinds in-

cluding lizard races, goat races, duck races, and even sheep races. However, horse racing is the most common event, and one of the biggest races is held in the first weekend in September in Birdsville.

Every year, this tiny town comes to life as more than five thousand people arrive for the Birdsville horse races. Stations from near and far bring their best horses for the national event, which has $110,000 in prize money for the winner. There is so much activity that the town engages air traffic controllers to regulate the hundreds of light aircraft that carry in the spectators. The weekend offers much unusual entertainment for visitors, including Fred Brophy's Boxing Troupe. This troupe is a traveling group of boxing professionals who compete with the local talent, and the

A Tour Guide's Life

With the growing number of tourists visiting the Outback, many town residents are becoming tour guides. Bill King was one of the first people in Central Australia to develop a tour guide business. In Rennie Ellis's book *We Live in Australia*, King describes the risks of his profession and the natural attributes of the Outback that draw travelers to his camping safaris:

"Australia is the driest continent on earth and traveling the vast unpopulated desert areas can be risky if you're not experienced and well-equipped. There are many tales of foolhardy travelers being stranded for days on some track after their car broke down. Some have died from thirst and heat exhaustion. It's always hot, but in the summer the temperature can reach [122 degrees] and more.

Australia is like six or seven countries in one, such is the difference in the terrain. As well as the deserts we take people through tropical rain forests, high alpine areas, and rolling plains carpeted with wild flowers. . . . The bird life is prolific. Australia has over 700 species of birds. Most people's favorites are the parrots and cockatoos, the birds of prey like the eagles, hawks and falcons, honey eaters, kingfishers, the laughing kookaburra, and the emu which is like an ostrich and can run 65 kilometers [forty miles] per hour. . . . There are all kinds of fascinating native animals, especially the marsupials, which carry their young in pouches. . . . Sometimes we visit Aboriginal settlements where the people's lives are still structured around the old tribal rituals and spiritual life. There are galleries of cave paintings thousands of years old. . . .

Outback Australia is a land of extremes. Nature is still the boss out here. It's the sense of space and freedom and the amazing harsh yet beautiful landscapes that attract the more adventurous traveler who comes on our camping safaris.

---

audience places bets on who will win the boxing rounds. The traveling boxers have colorful names like "Mad Dingo," and male members of the crowd are urged to test their skill and bravado against them. One journalist says, "There's always a few blokes drunk enough to try a few rounds against the professionals, and no shortage of others who will pay them to try."[117]

Employment

The lives of the townsfolk are also attuned to the seasons. People in Outback towns hold diverse jobs, many of which promote tourism. They generally work in local government, run small businesses, or work in tourist-related industries as motel managers, restaurant owners, tour guides, entertainers, bus drivers, and souvenir store owners. During the winter tourist season, plenty of these jobs are available, but in summer many residents leave town to escape the heat or to find employment elsewhere.

With their jobs and with other aspects of their lives, Outback town residents are flexible. They have to be, for the fortunes of the towns can change with shifts in the economy. Thus, many people have more than one job and frequently change their jobs to respond to changes in the market.

Since tourism is so popular in many Outback towns today, people are moving into jobs related to the growing tourist market. For example, Simone Lienert, who lives in Alice Springs, runs an Aboriginal-arts-and crafts retail store. To increase her income, she conducts tours for German tourists to Australia's most famous tour destination, Uluru or Ayer's Rock, a huge rock located in the center of Australia that holds spiritual significance for the Aborigines.

To further promote tourism in their towns, some town residents have come up with unique and creative tourist attractions. Many of these attractions capitalize on the country's unique history and culture. For example, the Tyrconnell mine in Queensland, a nineteenth-century gold mining town, is being reborn as a tourist attraction, revived and restored into a working gold mine. In Richmond, Queensland, Outback resident Robert Ievers found an ancient fossil of a giant marine reptile and became fascinated with the reptiles, dinosaurs, and prehistoric fish that once lived in the shallow inland sea that covered the town 10 million years ago. In 1999 Ievers founded the Richmond Reptile Fossil Museum, which has put Richmond on the tourist circuit and boosted the town's economy. And Outback resident Malcolm Douglas, who saw tourist potential in people's fascination with crocodiles, opened a crocodile farm in the 1980s near Broome in Western Australia. There he hatches hundreds of young crocodiles and gives talks to tourists on every aspect of crocodile life.

A tour guide stands ready with his tour bus in the Kimberley region. Tourism has become a profitable industry as interest in the Outback has risen.

Long Hours and Lots of Responsibility

Although most residents enjoy the lives they lead in Outback towns, there are some drawbacks. During the tourist season, these include long hours and the responsibility of looking after so many guests. Suzanne Stahmer from Helenvale says, "From April to September it's common to have three hundred vehicles through each day. We live here, we work here, we party here and we don't often get away."[118]

Long hours combined with the need to be responsible for other people at all times of the day or night means the tourist business requires a major commitment. Craig Catchlove says:

> Those in the business will not sing its praises as an easy life. . . . When you're dealing with tourists, it's seven days a week. You probably start around 4 A.M. . . . You've got to be married to your business. . . . If something goes wrong you need to be there. A vehicle breaks down in the middle of nowhere, what do you do at 3 A.M.? Find an alternate vehicle or take a part to them maybe [three hundred miles] away. . . . It [tourism] is a commitment you can't take lightly.[119]

Life in the off-season in Outback towns can be difficult as well. From October to May, temperatures soar over the one-hundred-degree mark, and the town populations are reduced to a fraction of their tourist season size. The rhythm of life abruptly changes. Says one Outback resident: "Summer months can be hell . . . our hottest day was 142 degrees in the shade . . . and we have really strong winds in November. I have [had to] shovel the dirt out of the doors with the dust storms we've had in the past."[120]

Under such conditions, problems in Outback towns sometimes escalate. For some residents, boredom and unemployment can lead to alcoholism, drug abuse, and crime. Keneally says violent crime statistics for many Outback towns are well above the national average: "The annual average for murders in the [Northern] Territory is fourteen times the Australian national mean; the prevalence of fire-arms, geographic remoteness, grievances germinating richly beneath the humid sun and fed on liquor, the high rate of individual eccentricity, the mysterious business of Aboriginal retribution—all that helps the figures along."[121]

Despite the increase in crime in some towns, for most Outback town residents, the off-season is welcomed as a time to rest and take it easy. The pressure is off, and they can relax, spend time with family members, and reconnect with the community. John Hammond of Mungerannie in Queensland says, "We have long lazy summers where we catch up on novels and letter-writing and doing things with the kids."[122] And in Birdsville residents say, "The off season is quiet tourist-wise so the townsfolk get together more because they have more time and more room to do so!"[123]

Outback Pubs

One place residents gather year-round is the local pub. Outback pubs are the hub of town social life. They are loud, vibrant places, often known for their unusual decor. For example, the walls of one pub, the Whim Creek Hotel in Western Australia, are decorated with dingo traps, newspaper clippings of mining booms and busts, and photos of cyclone destruction. The pub in Pyengana in Outback Tasmania sits in the middle of a paddock with its 350-pound resident pig called Slops, who can drink a bottle of beer in under five seconds.

A Taste of Real Outback Life

Tourists come from all over the world to towns in the Australian Outback. When they get there, many visitors want to experience life on Outback stations. For their part, station owners are taking advantage of this interest, particularly when droughts and low prices for wool and beef threaten their livelihood. All over the Outback, shearing sheds are being converted into guest quarters and paddocks into entertainment areas as station owners gear their operations to host large numbers of visitors during the tourist season.

Stations offer guests a range of activities. These include horse and motorbike riding, helping with mustering sheep and cattle, harvesting, hay making, or shearing. Some stations offer helicopter rides, rides in mustering planes, and camel treks through Outback country. And accommodations range from elegant old homesteads that have been converted into tourist bungalows, to rough shearing sheds or camping in swags (bedrolls) under the stars.

While some stations have converted their entire operation to tourism, most station owners juggle the demands of running the station with looking after guests. For most Outback families, tourism is just one more adaptation to change required of people living in the harsh Outback conditions.

A couple tours a sheep station in the Outback.

Visitors at an Outback pub find unusual food, plenty of cold beer, and a novel decor to enhance their experience.

In these unusual environments, pubs foster a special atmosphere that attracts people from all walks of life and encourages them to become friends. Art Linkletter describes his visit to a pub in Western Australia:

[Pubs] are always jam-packed with drinkers, animation and raucous enjoyment. So it was in the pub of the [town of] Grace Darling. Many of the Aussies were newcomers to town, some of them were blokes looking for an easy buck. There were stockmen from as far as four hundred miles away, and there were workers from the goldfields at Coolgardie and Kalgoorlie. There were men off the fishing boats and drifters from down east, and then there were the farmers, the sheepmen, the drovers and well-drillers. . . . As the suds [beer] went down so did the inhibitions and before long everybody in the place was slapping someone on the back and making like old friends.[124]

While people drink and talk with friends, they often develop a good appetite. Thus pubs offer hearty Outback dishes in generous proportions. Standard menu items include steak and eggs, meat pies, and french fries. Tourist interest in novel cuisine, however, has led to more adventurous alternatives. The Koetong Pub, for example, offers crocodile kebabs, kangaroo steaks, emu sausages, and grilled octopus, and in pubs throughout Central Australia, wild camel burgers and pies are becoming popular dishes.

Pubs also offer entertainment. Australians are great gamblers who love to bet on everything from horse races to dart games. Writer George Johnston says Australians will gamble on "far away race meetings, the fall of coins, the run of cards in a pack, the passage of two bull ants across a log or the color of a barmaid's underwear."[125] They are also avid players of a game called two-up. In two-up, a referee takes bets on whether two tossed coins will fall heads or tails up. The coins are thrown very rapidly, and large amounts of money exchange hands in record time. Linkletter describes his experience:

> We all gathered in a circle and one Aussie, . . . elected himself "ringer," which means referee. . . . For his services the ringer gets ten percent of the bets. One player, called the spinner, was handed a small board on which had been placed . . . two coins. The heads of the coins had been burnished so that they were shining, while the tail sides had been left dull. Before the spinner tossed the coins we all made bets . . . on whether the [coins] would fall heads or tails up. I was flabbergasted with the rapidity with which the bets were laid and the follow-through of the ringer calling for the spinner to toss the coins. The latter did this by holding his arm and the board at full length above his head and tossing the [coins] so that they spun before hitting the ground.[126]

Some pubs feature unusual attractions designed to draw patrons. Terry O'Hanlon's Great Western Pub in Rockhampton is one such place. Otherwise known as Rocky's Rodeo pub, O'Hanlon's has a rodeo ring at the back of the pub where up to three thousand spectators watch bull-riding competitions. Contestants take on beasts with names like "Danger Zone"

and "Smash." Massive horns from bulls that have met their demise hang from the pub's rafters. Other pubs offer quieter entertainment. The Lion's Den in Helenvale in far north Queensland has weekly sausage sizzles, and for New Year's Eve the pub hosts a boisterous party. Pub owner Suzanne Stahmer describes the event: "About five hundred people turned up and it went on for three days. . . . We had two bands, Fijian dancing, a talent quest and a big fire-works display. . . . Just a group of people having a great time. That, after all, is what a pub should be about."[127]

Loyalty and Fun

Giving people a good time is the focus of Outback pubs and much of town life in general. Outback people have a tremendous spirit of fun and great senses of humor. These qualities unite the residents and create a strong sense of community and immense loyalty to Outback towns. Says the mayor of Alice Springs, "There is an enthusiasm here . . . a sense of pride in the community . . . a tremendous attachment to place. . . . People do care what happens here. . . . There's a [tremendous] loyalty to Outback towns."[128]

This loyalty encourages inventiveness and results in the many varied events, activities, and business enterprises that draw large crowds, provide employment, and keep the towns afloat. Residents are motivated in these endeavors by their love of the Outback, a love that includes both the land and its people. "There's some sort of magic here that's hard to explain," says Nick Cummins, who runs a tourist venture in a remote Outback town. "The topography, the climate, . . . the sense of community are all part of it."[129] Jan McClure from Outback New South Wales agrees. In the end, she says, "It's the people that make the Outback."[130]

Notes

Introduction: Different People, Different Lives

1. Paul Myers, Editorial, *Outback Magazine*, October/November 1998, p. 1.
2. Thomas Keneally, *Outback*. Sydney: Hodder and Stoughton, 1983, pp. 42–46.
3. Quoted in Melissa McCord, *Outback Women*. Lane Cove, New South Wales: Doubleday, 1986, p. 39.
4. Terry Underwood, *Riveren, My Home, Our Country*. Sydney: Bantam Books, 2000, p. 72.

Chapter 1: An Ancient People

5. Ronald Berndt, "A Profile of Good and Bad in Australian Aboriginal Religion," in Max Charlesworth, ed., *Religious Business: Essays on Australian Aboriginal Spirituality*. Cambridge, UK: Cambridge University Press, 1998, p. 28.
6. Irene Watson, "Society," in Denis O'Byrne, ed., *Aboriginal Australia and the Torres Strait Islanders*. Melbourne: Lonely Planet, 2001, p. 106.
7. Jen Gibson, "Digging Deep," in Peggy Brock, ed., *Women's Rites and Sites*. Sydney: Allen and Urwin, 1989, p. 64.
8. Mudrooroo, *Aboriginal Mythology*. California: Aquarian, 1994, p. 145.
9. Labumore (Elsie Roughsey), *An Aboriginal Mother Tells of the Old and the New*. Victoria, Australia: Penguin Books of Australia, 1984, p. 83.
10. W.E. Harney, *Content to Lie in the Sun*. Sydney: Robert Hale, 1965, pp. 155–56.
11. Geoffrey Blainey, *Triumph of the Nomads*. New York: Woodstock Press, 1976, p. 131.
12. Labumore, *An Aboriginal Mother*, p. 61.
13. Mudrooroo, *Aboriginal Mythology*, p. 20.
14. Rosemary van den Berg, "Food-Bush Tucker," in Denis O'Byrne, ed., *Aboriginal Australia*, p. 99.
15. Quoted in Jennifer Isaacs, *Bush Food: Aboriginal Culture and Society*. Canberra: Aboriginal and Torres Strait Islander Commission, 1997, p. 10.
16. Quoted in Robert Tonkinson, *The Mardu Aborigines: Living the Dream in Australia's Desert*. Chicago: Holt, Rinehart, and Winston, 1991, p. 118.
17. Labumore, *An Aboriginal Mother*, pp. 50–51.
18. Labumore, *An Aboriginal Mother*, p. 62.
19. Labumore, *An Aboriginal Mother*, p. 91.
20. Tonkinson, *The Mardu Aborigines*, p. 59.
21. Carol Morse Perkins, *The Sound of Boomerangs*. New York: Atheneum, 1974, p. 69.
22. Manadawuy Yunupingu, "Reconciling with Aboriginality and Culture," www.yothuyindi.com.au, p. 1.
23. Baldwin Spencer and F.J. Gillen, in Hans Mol, *The Form and the Formless: Religion and Identity in Aboriginal Australia*. Canada: Wilfred Laurier University Press, 1982, p. 32.
24. Quoted in T.G.H. Strehlow, *Aranda Traditions*. Melbourne: Melbourne University Press, 1947, p. 116.
25. Labumore, *An Aboriginal Mother*, p. 89.
26. Quoted in A.W. Reed, *Aboriginal Life*. Sydney: A.H. and A.W. Reed, 1969, p. 124.
27. Yunupingu, "Reconciling with Aboriginality and Culture," p. 2.

Chapter 2: Cattle Mustering and Sheep Shearing

28. Underwood, *Riveren*, p. 47.
29. Terry Underwood, *In the Middle of Nowhere*, Sydney: Bantam Books, 1998, p. 132.
30. Debbie Dowden, "Aerial Stockmen," *Outback Magazine*, April/May 2001, p. 130.
31. Quoted in John Andersen, *Bagmen Millionaires: Life and People in Outback Queensland*. Victoria: Viking O'Neil, 1984, p. 25.
32. Keneally, *Outback*, p. 97.
33. Colin Stone, *Running the Brumbies: True Adventures of a Modern Bushman*. Sydney: Rigby, 1979, p. 41.
34. Rachel Smith, "The Bull Catchers," *Outback Magazine*, April/May 2000, p. 101.
35. Fiona Lake, "The Barkly's Classy Brunette," *Outback Magazine*, February/March 2001, p. 65.
36. Art Linkletter, *Linkletter Down Under*. Englewood Cliffs, NJ: Prentice-Hall, 1968, p. 147.
37. Darrell Taylor, "Shearer," in Phil Thornton and Paul Jones, *It's Only a Job*. Sydney: New Holland Publishers, 2000, p. 45.
38. Quoted in "Shear Outback: The Australian Shearer's Hall of Fame." www.shearoutback.com.au.
39. Matthew Cawood, "Shear Outback," *Australian Geographic*, January–March, 1998, p. 60.
40. Jill Ker Conway, *The Road from Coorain*. New York: Alfred Knopf, 1989, pp. 44–45.
41. Margaret Rau, *Red Earth, Blue Sky: The Australian Outback*. New York: Thomas Y. Crowell, 1981, p. 57.
42. Linkletter, *Linkletter Down Under*, p. 149.
43. Quoted in Chris Rowett and Selina Baxter, *To Ring the Shed*. Western Australia: Fremantle Arts Centre Press, 1995, p. 175.
44. Rowett and Baxter, *To Ring the Shed*, p. 18.
45. Underwood, *Riveren*, p. 71.

Chapter 3: At Home on the Station

46. Quoted in Kelly Penfold, "Saltbush Survivors," *Outback Magazine*, October/November 2000, p. 56.
47. Quoted in McCord, *Outback Women*, p. 38.
48. Andersen, *Bagmen Millionaires*, pp. 18–19.
49. Quoted in D.C. Money, *Australia Today*. New York: Cambridge University Press, 1989, p. 27.
50. Quoted in Amanda Burdon, "The Mail Run," *Australian Geographic*, January–March 1998, p. 61.
51. Burdon, "The Mail Run," p. 69.
52. Quoted in "World's Longest Mail Run," *Outback Magazine*, December/January 1999, p. 59.
53. Quoted in Peter Olszewski, "The Flying Doctor," *Outback Magazine*, April/May 1999, p. 37.
54. Quoted in Money, *Australia Today*, p. 30.
55. Marie Mahood, *Icing on the Damper*. Rockhampton, Queensland: Central University of Queensland Press, 1996, p. 166.
56. McCord, *Outback Women*, p. 15.
57. Quoted in Patty Mann, "It's Women's Work," *Outback Magazine*, April/May 2000, p. 39.
58. Underwood, *Riveren*, p. 10.

59. Conway, *Road from Coorain*, p. 41.
60. Quoted in Andersen, *Bagmen Millionaires*, p. 140.
61. Underwood, *Riveren*, p. 71.

Chapter 4: School by Air

62. Chris Tudor, interview with author, Alice Springs, September 11, 2001.
63. Quoted in Keneally, *Outback*, p. 129.
64. Underwood, *In the Middle of Nowhere*, p. 122.
65. Geoff O'Mallee, Alice Springs School of the Air presentation, September 7, 2001.
66. Underwood, *In the Middle of Nowhere*, p. 130.
67. Underwood, *In the Middle of Nowhere*, p. 244.
68. Quoted in Underwood, *In the Middle of Nowhere*, p. 160.
69. Quoted in Keneally, *Outback*, p. 130.
70. Geoff O'Mallee, e-mail to author, October 30, 2001.
71. *Alice Springs School of the Air*, "Communication." www.assoa.nt.edu.au, p. 2.
72. Lyn Conway, interview with author, King's Creek Station, September 5, 2001.
73. Conway, interview with author.
74. *National Enquiry into Rural and Remote Education*. Sydney: Commonwealth of Australia, 2000, p. 18.
75. Liz Tier, interview with author, Alice Springs, September 10, 2001.
76. Underwood, *In the Middle of Nowhere*, p. 152.
77. Alice Springs School of the Air Publication, p. 22.
78. Quoted in Liz Thompson, *Fighting for Survival*. Port Melbourne, Victoria: Heineman Library, 1998, p. 23.
79. O'Mallee, Alice Springs School of the Air presentation.
80. Quoted in Trisha Dixon, "The extraordinary Emmotts," *Outback Magazine*, April/May 1999, p. 40.
81. Underwood, *In the Middle of Nowhere*, p. 193.
82. Conway, *Road from Coorain*, p. 87.
83. Rau, *Red Earth, Blue Sky*, p. 17.
84. Tudor, interview with author.

Chapter 5: Opal Fever

85. Patrick O'Brien, "Opal Mania," *Australian Gold, Gem and Treasure*, January/February. 2000, p. 38.
86. Robert G. Haill, *Opals of the Never Never*. Kenthurst, New South Wales: Kangaroo Press, 1995, p. 22.
87. Archie Kalokerinos, *In Search of Opal*. Sydney: Ure Smith, 1967, p. 78.
88. Quoted in Rusty Bowen, *Miners' Tales from the Black Opal City*. Lightning Ridge, New South Wales: Bell's Ready Print, 1997, p. 65.
89. Marc Llewellyn, "Lightning Ridge," *Australian Geographic*, July–September 1998, p. 42.
90. Quoted in Bowen, *Miners' Tales*, p. 61.
91. Haill, *Opals of the Never Never*, p. 22.
92. Haill, *Opals of the Never Never*, p. 22.
93. Stephen Aracic, *Rediscover Opals—in Australia*. Underwood, Queensland: Kingswood Press, 1999, p. 43.
94. Haill, *Opals of the Never Never*, p. 92.
95. Peter Blythe, interview with author, Canberra, July 23, 2001.
96. Ann Blythe, interview with author, Canberra, July 23, 2001.
97. Quoted in Bowen, *Miners' Tales*, p. 51.
98. Quoted in Bowen, *Miners' Tales*, p. 57.
99. Haill, *Opals of the Never Never*, p. 24.
100. Patricia Gregory, "Opal-Hearted Country," www.patsopals.com.au, p. 1.
101. Haill, *Opals of the Never Never*, p. 124.

102. Quoted in Stephen Aracic, *Fortunes in Australian Opals*. Parramatta, New South Wales: Macarthur Press, 1988, p. 151.
103. Ann Marie Blythe, "Life in Mintabie: A Woman's View of the Opal Fields," *Australian Gem and Treasure Hunter*, no. 88, March 1984, p. 41.
104. Fred Ward, *Opals*. Bethesda, MD: Gem Book Publishers, 1997, p. 10.
105. Aracic, *Rediscover Opals*, p. 64.
106. Peter Blythe, interview with author.
107. Peter Blythe, interview with author.
108. Peter Blythe, "Mintabie Opal Fever," *Australian Gem and Treasure Hunter*, October 1982, p. 41.
109. Quoted in Llewellyn, "Lightning Ridge," p. 34.

Chapter 6: Outback Town Life

110. Jocelyn Burt, *Alice Springs*, Adelaide: Rigby, 1976, p. 4.
111. Margrit Beemster, "Watering Holes of the Upper Murray," *Outback Magazine*. December/January 2002, p. 118.
112. Craig Catchlove, interview with author, Alice Springs Tourist Bureau, September 11, 2001.
113. Fran Erlich, interview with author, Alice Springs, September 13, 2001.
114. Burt, *Alice Springs*, p. 2.
115. Burt, *Alice Springs*, p. 2.
116. Keneally, *Outback*, pp. 162–63.
117. Quoted in Melissa McCord, "Fred's Fighting for Cracow," *Outback Magazine*, February/March 2001, p. 28.
118. Quoted in Kirsty McKenzie, "Loitering in the Lion's Den," *Outback Magazine*, June/July 2000, p. 90.
119. Catchlove, interview with author.
120. Lyn Conway, interview with author, King's Creek Station, September 5, 2001.
121. Keneally, *Outback*, p. 79.
122. Quoted in Trisha Dixon, "On Track to Mungerannie," *Outback Magazine*, October/November 2000, p. 113.
123. E-mail to author from Birdsville, March 13, 2002.
124. Linkletter, *Linkletter Down Under*, pp. 65–67.
125. Linkletter, *Linkletter Down Under*, p. 75.
126. Linkletter, *Linkletter Down Under*, pp. 70–73.
127. Quoted in McKenzie, "Loitering in the Lion's Den," p. 91.
128. Erlich, interview with author.
129. Quoted in Amanda Ducker, "Re-inventing Nundle," *Outback Magazine*, June/July 2000, pp. 96–97.
130. Jan McClure, in Steve Meacham, "No Mallee Bull, the Outback Is Out There," *Sydney Morning Herald*, October 18, 2001, p. 5.

Glossary

The following list includes meanings of common words and expressions used in the Australian Outback. Many of the unusual terms and phrases reflect the region's casual and humorous culture.

arvo: Afternoon.

back o'Bourke: Back of beyond, middle of nowhere.

barbie: Barbecue.

bastard: General term of address that can be a good-natured form of greeting ("G'day, you old bastard"), a high level of praise ("He's the bravest bastard I know"), or a dire insult ("You lousy, lying bastard").

battler: One who tries hard, who struggles; the Outback is full of great Aussie battlers.

beaut, beauty: Great, fantastic.

billabong: Water hole in dried-up riverbed.

billy: A tin pot used to boil tea in the Outback.

bloke: Man.

blowies: Blowflies.

bludger: A lazy person who lives off other people.

blue: To have a blue, to have an argument.

bonzer: Great.

boomer: Large male kangaroo.

boomerang: A curved flat wooden tool used for hunting by Aborigines.

brumby: Wild horse.

bush: Country, anywhere away from the city.

bushranger: Australia's equivalent of the outlaws of the American Wild West.

bush tucker: Food available from plants and animals in the bush.

camp draft: Australian rodeo.

camp oven: Large cast-iron pot with lid, used for cooking over an open fire.

chook: Chicken.

cocky: Small-scale farmer.

come good: Turn out all right.

cooee: Within shouting distance, close by.

crook: Ill, badly made.

damper: Bush loaf made from flour and water and cooked in a camp oven.

didgeridoo: Wooden instrument played by Aborigines.

dingo: Indigenous wild dog.

dinky-di: The real thing.

Dog Fence: The world's longest fence used to keep dingoes out of southeast Australia.

droving: Moving livestock over large distances.

Dry (the): Dry season in the north of Australia.

dugout: A home built underground found in some Outback mining towns.

dunny: Outdoor toilet.

fair crack of the whip!: Fair go!

fair go!: Give me a break!

g'day: Traditional Australian greeting.

gibbers: Reddish-brown pebbles and boulders found on and near opal fields.

good on ya: Well done.

grazier: Large-scale sheep or cattle farmer.

grog: Alcoholic drinks.

homestead: The residence of a station owner.

how ya goin'?: How are you?

humpy: Aboriginal bark hut.

jackeroo: Young male trainee station manager.

jillaroo: Young female trainee on station.

jocks: Men's underpants.

joey: Young kangaroo or wallaby.

kiwi: A New Zealander.

knackered: Exhausted, tired.

knock: Criticize or deride.

lamington: Sponge cake covered with chocolate and coconut icing.

lollies: Candy.

mad as a cut snake: Insane, crazy.

mate: General term of familiarity.

mob: Herd of cattle or sheep while droving.

mulga: Arid zone acacia bush.

muster: Round up livestock.

never-never: A place very remote.

no-hoper: Hopeless case.

noodling: Searching for precious opal that has been missed by miners.

no worries: She'll be right, that's OK.

opal: Precious multicolored gem made from silica deposits.

Oz: Australia.

pastoralist: Large-scale grazier.

postie: Mail carrier.

potch: Common opal; colorless opal with the same texture as opal but of no value.

reckon!: You bet!

ripper: Good, great.

road train: Semitrailer with several trailers attached.

sanger: Sandwich.

sheila: Sometimes derogatory term for a woman.

she'll be right: It's OK, all will be well.

shoot through: Leave in a hurry.

shout: Buy a round of drinks.

singlet: Sleeveless shirt, worn by sheep shearers.

smoko: Tea break.

snag: Sausage.

spunky: Attractive, good-looking, bright and perky.

squatter: Pioneer grazier who rented land from the government.

station: Large sheep or cattle farm.

stickybeak: Nosy person.

strine: Australian slang.

swag: Canvas-covered bedroll used in the Outback.

swagman: Itinerant worker carrying his possessions in a swag.

ta: Thanks.

tea: Evening meal.

thingo: Thing, watchamacallit, dooverlacky, thingamijig.

tinny: Can of beer.

Top End: Northern part of the Northern Territory.

trucky: Truck driver.

true blue: Real or dinkum.

tucker: Food.

two-up: Traditional heads/tails gambling game played in pubs.

ute: Utility, pickup truck.

walkabout: Lengthy walk away from it all.

Wet (the): Rainy season in the north.

whinge: Complain or moan.

willy-willy: Whirlwind, dust storm.

wowser: Spoil sport, puritan.

woomera: Aboriginal spear-thrower.

yahoo: Noisy or unruly person.

yonks: Ages, a long time.

For Further Reading

Books

Rusty Bowen, *Miners' Tales from the Black Opal City*. Lightning Ridge, New South Wales: Bell's Ready Print, 1997. Opal miners from Lightning Ridge tell their stories in this spirited collection of interviews with the author.

Jocelyn Burt, *Australia's Outback*. Milton, Queensland: Jacaranda Wiley Press, 1992. A pictorial account of Australia's Outback country.

Susan Cottam, *Jillaroo: Station Life in the Outback*. Victoria, Australia: Penguin Books, 1990. A lively account of the life of a "jillaroo," a young female stock hand, as told in detailed letters home relating her experiences working on several Outback stations.

Max Griffiths, *Straight from the Heart: Tales of Tragedy and Triumph from the Nurses of the Australian Outback*. East Roseville, New South Wales: Simon and Schuster, 2000. Griffiths presents the nurses' own stories based on their reports back to base, which not only detail medical dramas but also present a down-to-earth picture of Outback life.

Mudrooroo, *Us Mob: History, Culture, Struggle: An Introduction to Indigenous Australia*. Pymble, New South Wales: Angus and Robertson, 1995. A leading Aboriginal activist writes about Aboriginal spirituality, relationships with the land, health, education, and law.

Boori (Monty) Pryor, *Maybe Tomorrow*. Ringwood, Victoria: Penguin Books, 1998. A young Aboriginal writer describes his family life and work with troubled Aboriginal teenagers in the Outback helping them reconnect to their traditional identity.

Chris Rowett and Selina Baxter, *To Ring the Shed*. Western Australia: Fremantle Arts Centre Press, 1995. The writer/photographer team interviewed hundreds of sheep shearers in the Outback in order to "give a feel for the working life of shearing teams . . . so that readers could see both the emotions and practical details of a shearer's day."

Bruce Simpson, *Hell, Highwater, and Hard Cases*. Sydney: ABC Books, 1999. Simpson was a stockman who dedicated this anthology of his poetry and true short stories to the memory of tough characters who helped tame the Outback.

Terry Underwood, *Riveren, My Home, Our Country*. Sydney: Bantam Books, 2000. Underwood writes about life on their remote family station in the Northern Territory in this book written for a young audience.

Website

Outback Magazine (www.outbackmag.com. au). Bimonthly magazine featuring articles on contemporary life in Australia's Outback, with features on stations, Outback pubs, towns, and profiles of people who live there.

Works Consulted

Books

K. Akerman, *Tools, Weapons, and Utensils.* Canberra: Aboriginal and Torres Strait Islander Commission, 1992. A description and explanation of traditional Aboriginal hunting tools and cooking utensils.

Jon Altman and Diane Smith, *Aboriginal People of the Northern Territory.* Canberra: Aboriginal and Torres Strait Islander Commission, 1998. Describes the history, religious beliefs, and life of the Aboriginal people today in the heart of the Outback.

John Andersen, *Bagmen Millionaires: Life and People in Outback Queensland.* Victoria: Viking O'Neil, 1984. In-depth descriptions, based on personal interviews, of the lives of people on a variety of Outback sheep and cattle stations.

Stephen Aracic, *Fortunes in Australian Opals.* Parramatta, New South Wales: Macarthur Press, 1988. An opal expert and Yugoslav migrant tells his story about catching "opal fever" and moving to Lightning Ridge.

———, *Rediscover Opals—in Australia.* Underwood, Queensland: Kingswood Press, 1999. A seasoned opal miner presents a comprehensive account of all aspects of opals and opal mining.

Geoffrey Blainey, *Triumph of the Nomads.* New York: Woodstock Press, 1976. Highly regarded Australian historian Geoffrey Blainey gives an insightful account of Aboriginal life and beliefs, which underscores their deep understanding of the Outback environment.

Peggy Brock, ed., *Women's Rites and Sites: Aboriginal Women's Cultural Knowledge.* Sydney: Allen and Unwin, 1989. A series of essays giving details on religious customs and ceremonies among Aboriginal women in the Outback.

Bill Bryson, *Down Under.* London: Doubleday, 2000. American writer Bill Bryson writes with wit and humor about his travels through the Australian Outback.

Jocelyn Burt, *Alice Springs*, Adelaide: Rigby, 1976. Burt describes life in one of the most famous towns in the heart of Australia's Outback.

Max Charlesworth, ed., *Religious Business: Essays on Australian Aboriginal Spirituality.* Cambridge, UK: Cambridge University Press, 1998. Essays on the merits of Aboriginal religion, Aboriginal women and religious expression, Aboriginal land rights, and other topics.

Jill Ker Conway, *The Road from Coorain.* New York: Alfred Knopf, 1989. Conway describes her journey from her girlhood on an isolated sheep station in New South Wales to her departure to the United States, where she eventually became president of Smith College.

R.M.W. Dixon, *Australian Languages.* Canberra: Aboriginal and Torres Strait Islander Commission, 1997. A history and description of Aboriginal languages.

Rennie Ellis, *We Live in Australia.* New York: The Bookwright Press, 1983. Designed for young audiences, this book includes brief autobiographical excerpts from Australian sheep shearers, teachers, doctors with the Royal Flying Doctor Service, Aboriginal elders, and others.

Sue and John Erbacher, *Life in the Outback*. Urangan, Queensland: John and Sue Erbacher Press, 1995. A general text for the juvenile market written by an ecologically minded couple who spent months traveling around the Outback.

Mrs. Aeneas Gunn, *We of the Never Never*. London: Hutchinson, 1908. A classic book on Outback life, written by the wife of a station owner about her life and adventures in the Outback at the turn of the twentieth century.

Robert G. Haill, *Opals of the Never Never*. Kenthurst, New South Wales: Kangaroo Press, 1995. An excellent source on opals and the life of the miners.

W.E. Harney, *Content to Lie in the Sun*. Sydney: Robert Hale, 1965. An in-depth look at Aboriginal life, by a man who married an Aborigine and spent most of his adult life working with Aborigines.

———, *Life Among the Aborigines*. London: Robert Hale, 1957. Harney lived among Aboriginal tribes for many years and describes their way of life with insight and empathy.

Ion Idriess, "Lighting Ridge," in *Ion Idriess's Greatest Stories: Of Mines and Soldiers*. North Ryde, New South Wales: Angus and Robertson, 1986. In writing about his experiences in the early part of the twentieth century, Idriess portrays the flavor of his life as an opal miner.

Jennifer Isaacs, *Bush Food: Aboriginal Culture and Society*. Canberra: Aboriginal and Torres Strait Islander Commission, 1997. Part of a series on Aboriginal culture, this government publication describes the traditional foods and food preparation practices of the Aborigines.

Archie Kalokerinos, *In Search of Opal*. Sydney: Ure Smith, 1967. A Greek doctor describes his passion for opal mining and his love of his life in a mining community.

Thomas Keneally, *Outback*. Sydney: Hodder and Stoughton, 1983. Australian author and novelist gives an evocative account of his travels into the Outback and his interaction with many Outback folk.

Labumore (Elsie Roughsey), *An Aboriginal Mother Tells of the Old and the New*. Victoria, Australia: Penguin Books of Australia, 1984. Autobiographical account of traditional Aboriginal life, attitudes, and changes in recent years.

Art Linkletter, *Linkletter Down Under*. Englewood Cliffs, NJ: Prentice-Hall, 1968. The American comedian details his firsthand experience of the trials and tribulations of trying to manage a profitable sheep station in Outback Western Australia.

Douglas Lockwood, *I the Aborigine*. Victoria: Ian Drakeford Publishing, 1988. Autobiographical work of an Aboriginal physician working with his people on the settlements.

Marie Mahood, *Icing on the Damper*. Rockhampton, Queensland: Central University of Queensland Press, 1996. The life story of an Outback family who lives on what has been called the most remote cattle station in all Australia.

Melissa McCord, *Outback Women*. Lane Cove, New South Wales: Doubleday, 1986. McCord gives first-person accounts of many Outback women and shows that women today face similar challenges to the pioneer women of early Australia.

Hans Mol, *The Form and the Formless: Religion and Identity in Aboriginal Australia*. Canada: Wilfred Laurier University Press, 1982. A collection of studies on Aboriginal religion, ethnic identity, and mythology.

D.C. Money, *Australia Today*. New York: Cambridge University Press, 1989. A description of Australia's geography, economy, and society targeted at a young audience.

Marlo Morgan, *Mutant Message from Down Under*. New York: Harper Collins, 1991. An American health worker tells the story of her fascinating experiences during a three-month journey traveling with a traditional Aboriginal tribe across the Outback.

Mudrooroo, *Aboriginal Mythology*. California: Aquarian, 1994. A well-known Aboriginal spokesman and poet defines many Aboriginal concepts.

National Enquiry into Rural and Remote Education. Sydney: Commonwealth of Australia, 2000. Report of a government inquiry evaluating the education system in Outback Australia.

Denis O'Byrne, ed., *Aboriginal Australia and the Torres Strait Islanders*. Melbourne: Lonely Planet, 2001. Written mainly by Aboriginal authors, the book describes the contemporary life of Australia's indigenous people in every state of the nation.

Carol Morse Perkins, *The Sound of Boomerangs*. New York: Atheneum, 1974. Perkins describes the life of a traditional nomadic Aboriginal tribe who live as hunters and gatherers.

Margaret Rau, *Red Earth, Blue Sky: The Australian Outback*: New York: Thomas Y. Crowell, 1981. The American author presents a straightforward account of many details of Outback life based on her journey around the Outback.

A.W. Reed, *Aboriginal Life*. Sydney: A.H. and A.W. Reed, 1969. Definitions and descriptions of Aboriginal religious and cultural practices and beliefs.

L. Satterthwait, *Hunting and Gathering*. Canberra: Aboriginal and Torres Strait Islander Commission, 1990. A description of traditional hunting and gathering practices of Australia's Aborigines.

Colin Stone, *Running the Brumbies: True Adventures of a Modern Bushman*. Sydney: Rigby, 1979. Stone spent nearly thirty years as a stockman in the Outback and in this lively autobiographical work gives a real flavor of life in the bush.

T.G.H. Strehlow, *Aranda Traditions*. Melbourne: Melbourne University Press, 1947. A highly reputed anthropologist presents a collection of essays on Aboriginal life and spirituality.

Liz Thompson, *Fighting for Survival*. Port Melbourne, Victoria: Heineman Library, 1998. The Aboriginal author describes modern-day life and attitudes of Aboriginal people to their past treatment and the future.

Phil Thornton and Paul Jones, *It's Only a Job*. Sydney: New Holland Publishers, 2000. Australians discuss their feelings about a variety of jobs, including working as sheep shearers and cattle drovers.

Robert Tonkinson, *The Mardu Aborigines: Living the Dream in Australia's Desert*. Chicago: Holt, Rinehart, and Winston, 1991. Life among an Aboriginal group who lives in the Gibson Desert of Western Australia.

Terry Underwood, *In the Middle of Nowhere*. Sydney: Bantam Books, 1998. This is a moving account of the ups and downs of home and family life on a remote cattle station in the Northern Territory.

Fred Ward, *Opals*. Bethesda, MD: Gem Book Publishers, 1997. Description of opal mining and life on the opal fields in major opal towns in Australia.

Periodicals

Margrit Beemster, "Watering Holes of the Upper Murray," *Outback Magazine*, December/January 2002.

Ann Marie Blythe, "Life in Mintabie: A Woman's View of the Opal Fields," *Australian Gem and Treasure Hunter,* no. 88, March 1984.

Peter Blythe, "Mintabie Opal Fever," *Australian Gem and Treasure Hunter*, October 1982.

Amanda Burdon, "The Mail Run," *Australian Geographic*, January–March 1998.

Matthew Cawood, "Shear Outback," *Australian Geographic*, January–March, 1998.

Liz Davis, "The dog fence man," *Outback Magazine*, October–November, 2000.

Trisha Dixon, "On Track to Mungerannie," *Outback Magazine*, October/November 2000.

———, "The Extraordinary Emmotts," *Outback Magazine*, April–May 1999.

Debbie Dowden, "Aerial Stockmen," *Outback Magazine*, April/May 2001.

Amanda Ducker, "Re-inventing Nundle," *Outback Magazine*, June/July 2000.

Fiona Lake, "The Barkly's Classy Brunette," *Outback Magazine*, February/March 2001.

Marc Llewellyn, "Lightning Ridge," *Australian Geographic*, July–September 1998.

Patty Mann, "It's Women's Work," *Outback Magazine*, April/May 2000.

Melissa McCord, "Fred's Fighting for Cracow," *Outback Magazine*, February/March 2001.

Kirsty McKenzie, "Loitering in the Lion's Den," *Outback Magazine*, June/July 2000.

———, "RAFS Girls Come Out to Play," *Outback Magazine*, October/November 1999.

Steve Meacham, "No Mallee Bull, the Outback Is Out There," *Sydney Morning Herald*, October 18, 2001.

Paul Myers, Editorial, *Outback Magazine*, October/November 1998.

Patrick O'Brien, "Opal Mania," *Australian Gold, Gem, and Treasure*, January/February 2000.

Peter Olszewski, "The Flying Doctor," *Outback Magazine*, April/May 1999.

Kelly Penfold, "Saltbush Survivors," *Outback Magazine*, October/November 2000.

Rachel Smith, "The Bull Catchers," *Outback Magazine*, April/May 2000.

"World's Longest Mail Run," *Outback Magazine*, December/January 1999.

Internet Sources

Patricia Gregory, "Opal-Hearted Country." www.patsopals.com.au.

Websites

Alice Springs School of the Air (www. assoa.nt.edu.au). The Northern Territory Education Department gives information on the School of the Air and schools in Outback towns.

The Australian Department of Foreign Affairs (www.dfat.gov.au). Includes a number of fact sheets on Australia and on Australia's indigenous people—for example, on where indigenous Australians live, on indigenous land rights, and on the mining industry and indigenous Australians.

The Northern Territories Tourist Commission (www.insidetheoutback.com). The Northern Territories Commission gives general information on the Outback with a number of useful link sites.

The Kooris (www.koori.usyd.edu.au). An informative site designed by the Kooris, an Aboriginal tribe from Western Australia; the site explains their culture, history, and way of life.

The Royal Flying Doctor Service (www.rfds.org.au). The website of the Royal Flying Doctor Service details its history and provides general information on the day-to-day operations of the medical service to the Outback.

The Australian Shearer's Hall of Fame. (www.shearoutback.com.au). The site of the Australian Shearer's Hall of Fame in New South Wales, which includes stories written by the shearers about their lives and work.

Yothu Yindi (www.yothuyindi.com). Yothu Yindi is an Aboriginal rock band that plays rock music with a mix of modern and traditional instruments like the didgeridoo. In their website they talk with insight about black/white relations and the strength of Aboriginal spiritual life.

Index

Picture Credits

Cover photo: © Penny Tweedy/CORBIS

Australian Tourist Commission, 21, 22, 30, 32, 34, 40, 43, 46, 47, 49, 51, 56, 59, 67, 84, 85, 86, 91, 92

©Yann Arthus-Bertrand/CORBIS, 36

©Bettmann/CORBIS, 25

©CORBIS, 10, 11, 20, 23, 37, 39, 44, 52, 81

Dirck Hasltead/Liaison/Getty Images, 78

Brandy Noon, 9

North Wind Picture Archives, 14

©Christine Osborne/CORBIS, 19

©Carl & Ann Purcell/CORBIS, 79

©David Samuel Robbins/CORBIS, 89

©Paul A. Souders/CORBIS, 13, 64, 70, 72, 76

©Penny Tweedy/CORBIS, 15, 16, 26, 62, 66

Lou Vicky/FDB/Liaison Agency, 68, 74, 75

©Patrick Ward/CORBIS, 60, 87

About the Author

In researching this book, Australian-born writer and editor Jann Einfeld camped in a swag under the Southern Cross and felt wonder in the stillness of vast round orange moons. True blue Outback folk taught her to listen to their spirit between, around, and under the words. For seven years she lived and worked on a remote ranch in Snowflake, Arizona, which was good training for writing this book. A varied life has included work in Third World countries with the Australian government and the World Bank, working in universities, writing children's books, and encouraging the creation of fine poetry in young children.